Praise for
TONY HILLERMAN
and
THE GREAT TAOS BANK ROBBERY

"Hillerman is surely one of the finest and
most original craftsmen at work . . . today."
—*Boston Globe Book Review*

"This collection is the
essence of Hillerman, which is always instructive fun."
—*New Mexican*

"What newcomers sometimes find irritating in the
general incompetency and charm of this capital of mañana,
Hillerman portrays with simple accuracy: it is hilarious."
—*Taos News*

"Deserves a wide readership . . . some of Hillerman's pieces
are classics . . . the kind of great writing that uses regional
commentary to explain what may be innate behaviors
in all Western humans."
—*Albuquerque Journal*

"Tony Hillerman is a wonderful storyteller."
—*New York Times Book Review*

BOOKS BY TONY HILLERMAN

Fiction

Hunting Badger

The First Eagle

The Fallen Man

Finding Moon

Sacred Clowns

Coyote Waits

Talking God

A Thief of Time

Skinwalkers

The Ghostway

The Dark Wind

People of Darkness

Listening Woman

Dance Hall of the Dead

The Fly on the Wall

The Blessing Way

The Boy Who Made Dragonfly (for children)

Nonfiction

Seldom Disappointed

Hillerman Country

New Mexico, Rio Grande and Other Essays

The Spell of New Mexico

Photograph by AP Newsfeatures

About the Author

TONY HILLERMAN is past president of Mystery Writers of America and has received their Edgar and Grand Master awards. His other honors include the Center for the American Indian's Ambassador Award, the Silver Spur Award for the best novel set in the West, the Navaho Tribe's Special Friend Award, the National Media Award from the American Anthropological Association, the Public Service Award from the U.S. Department of the Interior, the Nero Wolfe Award, the Lifetime Achievement Award from the Oklahoma Center for the Book, Honorary Life Membership in the Western Literature Association, and the Grand Prix de Litterature Policiere. In addition to his election to Phi Beta Kappa, Tony Hillerman has been named Doctor of Humane Letters at Arizona State University and at Portland University. He lives with his wife, Marie, in Albuquerque, New Mexico.

THE
GREAT TAOS
BANK ROBBERY

AND OTHER TRUE STORIES
OF THE SOUTHWEST

TONY HILLERMAN

Perennial

An Imprint of HarperCollinsPublishers

This book was originally published in 1973 by the University of New Mexico Press.

HarperCollins books may be purchased for educational, business, or sales promotional use. For information please write: Special Markets Department, HarperCollins Publishers Inc., 10 East 53rd Street, New York, NY 10022.

First Perennial edition published 2001.

Library of Congress Cataloging-in-Publication Data

Hillerman, Tony.
    [Great Taos bank robbery and other Indian country affairs]
    The great Taos bank robbery and other true stories of the Southwest / Tony Hillerman.
        p. cm.
    Originally published in 1973 as: The great Taos bank robbery and other Indian country affairs.
    ISBN 0-06-093712-2 (pbk.)
    1. New Mexico—History—Anecdotes. 2. New Mexico—Biography—Anecdotes. I. Title.
F796.6 .H54 2001
978.9—dc21

                                                    2001036078

01   02   03   04   05   NK/RRD   10   9   8   7   6   5   4   3   2   1

For Marie

Acknowledgments

Several of the chapters in this book have been previously published, in forms ranging from very similar to drastically modified, by magazines and periodicals. "The Great Taos Bank Robbery," "The Very Heart of Our Country," "Las Trampas," "Othello in Union County," and "The Conversion of Cletus Xywanda" all appeared, in one form or another, in *New Mexico Magazine*. The magazine's editor, Walter Briggs, and members of his staff were also involved in germinating the idea which led to this volume. Other material included here previously appeared in modified form in *True*, the *Western Review*, or the *New Mexico Quarterly*.

Contents

THE
GREAT TAOS
BANK ROBBERY

1

The Great Taos Bank Robbery

The Newsroom of The New Mexican first got word of the incident about ten minutes after nine the morning of November 12, 1957. Mrs. Ruth Fish, who had served for many years as manager of the Taos Chamber of Commerce and almost as many as Taos correspondent for the Santa Fe newspaper, called collect and asked for the city editor.

She told the city editor that the Taos bank would be robbed that morning. She said that she would walk over to the bank and watch this operation. She promised to call in an eyewitness account before the first edition deadline at 11:00 A.M.

The city editor asked how Mrs. Fish knew the bank was to be robbed. Mrs. Fish, in a hurry to get off the telephone and become an eyewitness, explained very briefly that one of her lady friends had stopped in her office and told her so. The lady was now waiting so that they could walk down together and watch.

But, the city editor insisted, how did the lady friend know the bank was to be robbed that morning?

Because, Mrs. Fish explained with patience, the two bank robbers were standing in line at this very moment waiting their turn at the teller's cage.

But, persisted the city editor, how was it possible to predict that these two persons intended to rob the bank?

This presumption seemed safe, Mrs. Fish said, because one of the two men was disguised as a woman and because he was holding a pistol under his purse. Whereupon she said good-bye and hung up.

While astonished by the foregoing, the city editor recalled later that he had no doubt at all that the bank would indeed be robbed in the fashion described. If the reader feels less sure at this point, it is because the city editor had two advantages. First, he knew Mrs. Fish. An elderly woman of dignity, charm, and grandmotherly appearance, she possessed a flawless reputation for accuracy. Second, he knew Taos. While bank robbers probably wouldn't stand politely in line with the paying customers in Omaha or Atlanta, there was no reason to believe they wouldn't in this peculiar little town.

As a matter of fact they were doing exactly this, and their courtliness was about to cause them trouble. The chain of events that followed did not reach its semifinal anticlimax until sixty hours later and was not officially ended until the following February, when the federal grand jury met sixty-five miles south in Santa Fe. By then the affair was being called The Great Taos Bank Robbery.

Lest the reader be misled by this title, he should be warned that Taos also lists in its litany of notable events The Great Flood of 1935. If the reader can accept the fact that Taos managed a Great Flood without a river and with the very modest amount of water available in its arid climate, he is prepared to hear more about what happened on November 12, 1957.

After the city editor collected his wits, he placed a long-distance call to the bank. The secretary who answered didn't know anything about any bank robbery, but she referred the call to a higher ranking official. The city editor asked this gentleman if his bank had been robbed. Certainly not, said the banker. How in the world did such rumors get started?

A few minutes later Mrs. Fish called back, slightly breathless. She reported that she and her friend had walked through the alley behind the Safeway store and arrived at the bank just as two men with drawn pistols dashed from the front door. One of the men was dressed as a woman, as previously reported. He ran awkwardly in his high heels. The two jumped into a green pickup truck parked in the alley and drove away. From what she had learned from spectators fortunate enough to arrive earlier, the two men had not taken any money from the bank. She would investigate further and call back. Mrs. Fish, a woman of impeccable courtesy, hung up without a word of reproach to the city editor for causing her to be late for the event.

The city editor now placed another call to the banker. He asked the banker if he was sure his bank hadn't been robbed, or something. The bank official now was less confident. He was sure nobody had taken any money but he was also sure that something funny had been going on. He had been hearing something about a man dressed as a woman, and two men running wildly out of the bank lobby, and other confusing stories.

Meanwhile, the police reporter had called the Taos police department and said he was checking on a rumor that there had been a bank robbery. The policeman who answered said no, there hadn't been one and he guessed the police would be the first to hear about it if there was one, wouldn't they? The reporter said yes, he guessed that was true. Actually, the police would be approximately the last to hear about it, being informed only after the pastor of the local United Brethren Church entered the picture.

By then Mrs. Fish had made her third call and provided the city editor with a detailed account of what had happened in the bank lobby. The two men had arrived just as the bank opened its doors at 9:00 A.M. They found a crowd of Taos businessmen waiting to check out funds to fuel their cash registers for the day. The suspects joined the rush to the tellers' cages but were outdistanced, perhaps because of the high heels, and were stuck well back in the line. Customers quickly noticed that the line-stander clad as a woman had a full day's growth of dark stubble bristling through his pancake makeup and that the nylons encased an unseemly growth of leg hair. They also noticed that this person's costume was remarkably *chic* for Taos, which is one of the few places where a man can still feel adequately dressed downtown in bib overalls. All this was enough to cause a modest amount of buzzing in the lobby, but probably not much. Taos is a tolerant village, well accustomed to whimsy. It has been said that if the late James Thurber had been raised here he would never have celebrated the antics of his family in print, since what seems outlandish in Columbus, Ohio, seems fairly normal in Taos. It is also said that if Sinclair Lewis had been a Taoseño, Babbit would have had a common-law wife and worn sandals. In Taos a certain amount of eccentricity is required for conformity.

Interest among the spectators quickened, however, when some of them saw—or thought they saw—a pistol in the hand of the pseudo-woman. The fleet-footed ones, who had beaten the rush to the tellers' windows and therefore left early, spread the news of this unusual sight around Taos Plaza. Thus did Mrs. Fish receive the word, and thus were many curious townfolks drawn to the bank to watch the spectacle.

Several days later, one of the two suspects was to complain to federal agents that some among this growing crowd of spectators began giggling. Whether or not Taos residents were guilty of such churlishness, the two young men soon began suffering from stage fright. Embarrassed by the scrutiny of the crowd, they fled from the bank just as Mrs. Fish and her friend were arriving.

It was definitely established finally that both men were armed with loaded pistols. Although they were not to use these weapons until later, and then only when cruelly provoked, these revolvers are important because they lend an air of reality to The Great Taos Bank Robbery. It was much the same with The Great Flood of 1935. While it wasn't a flood in the usual definition, people actually did get wet and Taoseños defend this historic event from scoffers by pointing out that Governor Clyde Tingley declared an emergency and scores of families were evacuated to the National Guard Armory.

These facts seem persuasive unless one knows that this Great Flood was actually an epidemic of leaking roofs—the combined effect of a freakishly slow and persistent rain and the traditional Taos habit of roofing flat-topped adobe buildings with hard-packed adobe clay. This roofing material is usually as effective as it is inexpensive, since Taos rainstorms are commonly brief, noisy, and productive of very little moisture. Taos learned in 1935 that when an Eastern-style three-day drizzle happens, such economical roofs tend to dissolve and pour through the ceilings. Residents, Taoslike, persist in using dirt roofs and profited from the experience only by the legends of bravery, charity, and outrageous discomfort that it created.

Today Taoseños rely on the two loaded pistols to lend authenticity to their Great Taos Bank Robbery just as they drag out the governor's unlocking of the armory when an outsider depreciates their flood. But before these pistols started going off, a couple of things had to happen.

As Mrs. Fish reported, the two suspects roared away from the scene of their fiasco in a pickup truck. Their rush may have been prompted by the erroneous notion that someone would call the police, or perhaps by sheer embarrassment. Whatever the cause, the two ran a stop sign and sideswiped a car driven by the United Brethren minister. The minister was not in the mood that morning to turn the other fender. He insisted that the accident be reported to the police and that neither vehicle be moved until an officer arrived. The suspects took a dissenting position and insisted on driving away. The reader is aware that they had good reason for this rudeness but the pastor at the moment was not. Neither could he know that the man in the pickup who wore lipstick and face powder had gotten himself up as a female for the relatively innocent purpose of misleading bank personnel. It is safe to guess that the minister suspected a darker purpose, since Taos has long been known as a place of confusion concerning gender. At any rate, when the two men drove away, the minister gave chase.

Taos is a small community and its streets are few, narrow, crooked, and short. It is a completely inappropriate setting for a high-speed automobile chase and offers limited opportunity for the chasees to elude the chaser. After two or three times around the village the two suspects must have faced the fact that there was no hope of shaking off their pursuer. They began firing their pistols at the minister's car. Thus discouraged, the minister stopped at a telephone and the police, at long last, learned that something was amiss in Taos.

This seeming lack of rapport between Taos and the forces of authority would not surprise those familiar with the history of the village. The attitude of Taoseños had been largely responsible in 1847 for a joint proposal by Secretary of State Daniel Webster and Secretary of War C. M. Conrad that the United States withdraw from the Territory of New Mexico and "allow it to revert to its native inhabitants." The Webster-Conrad discouragement seems to have been due in large part to the fact that the townspeople of Taos, in a cooperative venture with the adjoining Taos Indian Pueblo, had scalped Territorial Governor Charles Bent. The residence where this unique impeachment occurred is still maintained by the village as a museum that, one suspects, celebrates the deed more than the martyr. On another and later occasion, U.S. Attorney W.W.H. Davis reported with disapproving sarcasm that the door of the Taos jail was "securely fastened with a twine string" and concluded that this lack of a bona fide lock might be why prisoners were so often missing when time came to try them. A person reading the Davis diary senses he might have had more to say on this subject had his attention not been diverted by conditions at the Pontius Pilate Hotel. Mr.

Davis had called the attention of the innkeeper to the lack of coverings on his bed and his host had corrected this deficiency by handing him the cloth from the dining table. Mr. Davis reported himself "somewhat exercised of mind" during the night with the question of how his host would supply the place of the table-cloth when morning came. When the sheet reappeared on the breakfast table, the U.S. attorney celebrated this ingenuity with a heroic couplet:

> *Thus it contrived the double debt to pay,*
> *A sheet by night—a table cloth by day.*

The Taos jail is now locked, but its walls are still made of adobe, which is vulnerable—as a prisoner named Danny Montoya recently demonstrated—to plastic spoons. Montoya spooned a hole through the wall but made two mistakes. First, he chose the wrong wall—digging his way into the county treasurer's office, which adjoins the lockup, instead of to freedom. Second, he underestimated his diameter, jammed himself into his exit route, and spent the night like a cork in a bottle with his head still in custody.

Aside from the jail, Taoseños' lack of interest in law enforcement can perhaps best be illustrated by an obituary article to which *El Crepusculo de Libertad,* a now-defunct Taos weekly newspaper, devoted two-thirds of its front pages in 1953. The obituary reported the death of John Dunn, a very prominent Taos resident. It noted that Mr. Dunn had arrived at Taos after making his way from the Texas State Penitentiary without benefit of pardon or parole and with thirty-nine years and six months left to serve on a forty-year sentence. It recounted Mr. Dunn's exploits as a dealer of two-card Monte and as operator of gambling establishments at Taos and elsewhere in the county. "John Dunn was at his best behind a roulette wheel or a Monte table, where you never got more than was coming to you and if you didn't watch it was less. I have seen John Dunn stand for ten hours at a roulette wheel and never look up, never asleep on the job, and never overlooking a chance to slip you a short stack of chips," the obituary writer reported.

Gambling is not legal in New Mexico. Nor, for that matter, is escaping from prison. Yet before John Dunn died in 1953 at the age of ninety-four, he had lived sixty-four years in Taos, had been in the public eye enough to have the John Dunn Bridge bear his name, and had not been molested by the law. One can only assume that, as in the case of The Great Taos Bank Robbery, police were slow in getting the word.

Once the police were belatedly informed of the doings of November 12, at the bank and elsewhere, they reacted with vigor. A search began immediately for the two suspects. The State Police were notified and the Federal Bureau of Investigation was told of the apparent affront to the Federal Banking Act. By noon, the population of Taos—normally about 1,850—had been swollen by the influx of various types of officers. In addition to the genuine gendarmes representing federal, state, county, and village governments, volunteer organizations such as the Mounted Patrol and Sheriff's Posse were mobilized.

Authorities soon had the escape vehicle. It was driven into the midst of a swarm of lawmen by Jose T. Cardenas. Mr. Cardenas, when he collected himself from the shock of having guns pointed at him, explained that he had lent his truck to a friend the previous day and that it had been left at his house that morning bearing signs of collision damage. Mr. Cardenas was at that moment in search of this friend to demand an explanation.

The reader might well pause here and recollect that it is traditional among robbers to steal escape vehicles, not to borrow them from friends. Borrowing, while more polite, leads to speedy identification when the car is recovered. Mr. Cardenas was able to tell police that he had loaned his truck to a man I shall call Joe Gomez, a thirty-three-year-old Taos native, and that Mr. Gomez was accompanied by Frederick Smith, a twenty-three-year-old resident of Maine who had been visiting in the village.

Police also quickly received a hint of why the two had borrowed the truck a day early. Witnesses were found who had seen them at the entrance of the bank the previous morning—the morning of November 11. The witnesses remembered this because they thought it odd to see a man dressed as a woman trying to get into the bank on Veterans' Day. If any doubts remained on the subject, this should have proved that the two were not professional bank bandits, since professionals presumably would know about national bank holidays.

At this point, the authorities appeared to be in an unusually happy position. They knew the identities of both men they sought. They had excellent descriptions of the suspects. They were confident both were afoot in Taos. The village is small, the lawmen were numerous, and there was every reason for confidence that the two culprits would be in custody in a very few minutes. The officers fanned out from the plaza to press their search.

This proved to be a mistake, because Gomez and Smith had decided to walk down to the plaza to try to borrow some money. While the federal, state, county, and city officers and their volunteer posses manned roadblocks and poked around in the outlying areas, the two fugitives were making a door-to-door canvass of downtown bars soliciting loans from the bartenders. Not unnaturally, the barkeeps considered the two as poor credit risks at the moment. By the time it occurred to someone to inform the law of this activity, Gomez and Smith had become discouraged and wandered off.

By the time the sun dipped behind the Conejos Mountains, the lawmen had found Gomez's female attire abandoned in an outdoor toilet but the fugitives were still at large. The hunt continued through the night, brightening the frosty November darkness with flashlights and electric lanterns. Considering the number of officers involved and the modest dimensions of Taos it is safe to guess that at least one policeman looked almost everywhere at least once, except in the deserted house where the two had chosen to sleep. When the sun rose over the Taos Mountains the morning of November 13, Gomez and Smith were still at large. There was some talk now of sending for Sam, the New Mexico bloodhound, but the motion apparently died for lack of a second. Perhaps this was because the only time Sam was used in Taos County he immediately became disoriented, strayed, and was lost for two days.

November 13 passed with a methodical and fruitless combing of the village. There was a brief flurry of excitement when officers learned in some roundabout manner that Gomez and Smith had again appeared on the plaza, renewing their futile attempts to float a loan. Police now discovered, twelve hours too late to do them any good, where Gomez and Smith had spent the previous night. They discovered that a neighborhood householder had happened by their hideout, had seen the fugitives, had stopped to chat with them about the excitement they had caused, and had then left to buy them some groceries. The reader by now will not be surprised to know that this good neighbor did not bother to notify the police. But he did play a little joke on the culprits when he returned with the food, telling them that they had critically wounded the minister and that officers had orders to get them dead or alive. This unnerving bit of misinformation drove the two to make their second return to the plaza the next morning to renew the attempt to borrow traveling money. While one can imagine that their pleas were eloquent, the bartenders remained adamant. Gomez told a reporter two days later that by now he and Smith were "feeling mighty blue."

If the fugitives were depressed by November 13, it is reasonable to bet that those involved in the search for them shared this feeling. Taos does not lend itself to extended manhunts, since the posse members soon run out of places to look. To make matters worse, the press had taken the matter lightly from the first and the newspaper irreverence increased as the search dragged. When November 14 wore on without a sign of the fugitives, those in charge of the hunt must have been casting about for a dignified excuse to call off the whole affair. Their ordeal, however, was almost over.

That night, a Taos resident named Nat Flores was lying on his bed reading the evening paper when he heard a tapping on his window. Outside he saw two young men whom he recognized as

Gomez and Smith. The two inquired if he might provide them with a meal and Flores, with typical "my house is your house" Taos hospitality, invited his visitors in for supper. During the meal, Flores and Joe V. Montoya, a brother-in-law who had stopped in for a chat, found Gomez and Smith in a gloomy mood. The two said they had spent the previous night in frostbitten discomfort in Kit Carson Park, a small recreation area not far from Taos plaza. One of the possemen, Smith complained, had almost stepped on his finger. Flores and Montoya, after a lengthy argument in which Flores recalled quoting passages from the Bible, persuaded the two that they should accept a ride down to the sheriff's office after supper and turn themselves in.

The final footnote on The Great Taos Bank Robbery was not written until February 4, 1958. After the surrender, officers found the two refreshingly frank about their activities. In due course, Joe Gomez and Frederick Smith were accused by the U.S. District Attorney of conspiring to violate the provisions of the Federal Banking Act and their case was placed on the winter docket for consideration by the Federal Grand Jury. Unfortunately, grand jury proceedings are secret so we will never know exactly what happened when the case was presented. We do know that the jury returned a "no bill," which indicates—at very least—that the jurors could not be convinced that Gomez and Smith took their pistols into the Taos bank with felonious intentions. If the jurors were not familiar with Taos, they may have suspected the FBI imagined the whole unlikely episode.

Thus The Great Bank Robbery was denied the official federal imprimatur of indictments and was left as the sort of thing Alice's Mad Hatter might call an Unfelonious Unrobbery.

Still, if you happen to be in Taos on Veterans' Day and the man on the next barstool happens to be an Old Taos Hand, you're likely to hear something like this:

"You know, tomorrow is the anniversary of our Big Bank Robbery."

Or maybe he'll tell you about The Great Flood of 1935.

The Navajo Who Had So Many Friends
He Couldn't Get No Wire Strung

The young matron who went to Barnard College and Read a Book Once is explaining to the Valencia County Wool Grower and me about Navajo mythology. "Snake was one of the Holy People who came up to the Earth Surface World with First Man and First Woman," she tells us, "which is why Navajos won't kill snakes."

Valencia County Wool Grower stops poking at the olive in his martini glass. "One time," he says, "I got Old Man Madman to get some of his sons-in-law and build some fence for me over there by Redondo Mesa. I warned him about all those rattlesnakes out there in the malpais, and he says, 'Dats all right. Snakes are frens of de Navajo.' So the next day I haul some wire out there and there's dead snakes laying all over that lava rock. So I says, 'Hosteen Madman, how come you told me rattlesnakes and Navajos are friends?' and he kinda grins and he says, 'We frens, but we had so goddam many frens around here we couldn't get no wire strung.'"

2

The Very Heart
of Our Country

We are standing, Alex Atcitty and I, on the slope under that great rampart of red rock which runs like a Chinese Wall along the south end of Navajo country. To the east, Mount Taylor rises snowcapped and serene above the blunt shape of Little Haystack Mountain. To the left, eroded sandstone, broken slate, and a half-dead piñon whose branches collect tumbleweeds from the gutsy wind. It is November of a year of almost unbroken drought. The air smells of autumn, pine resin, dust, and empty places. The only living things in sight are a sparrow hawk and a disconsolate Hereford. The hawk is scouting the rim of the red mesa for incautious rodents. The cow, resting from its search for something to eat, is staring moodily in the direction of Gallup.

"You know," Attcitty says, "they gave us our choice. A bunch of rich Arkansas River bottomland over in Oklahoma or this."

He waves his arm, including erosion, dead brush, cow, and an infinity of gaudy sunset sky in the gesture, and grins at me. "When you understand why we picked this rock pile instead of that thousand-dollar-an-acre cotton land, then you understand Navajos."

The Navajos made this historic choice on May 28, 1868. It had been offered the day before by General William Tecumseh Sherman to Barboncita, Manuelito, Ganado Mucho, and other clan leaders. In return for their pledge never again to bear arms, the U.S. government would give them a choice of reservations. They could remain at Fort Sumner, where most of them had been unhappily penned since 1864, or the government would transport them to a well-watered, well-timbered, game-rich reservation in the Arkansas River Valley of Indian Territory. As a third alternative, they could return to that arid expanse of canyons and mesas from which the Army had starved them by a three-year campaign of hogan burning, cattle killing, and general earth scorching. In his report to President Andrew Johnson, General Sherman made it clear the land involved in this third choice was worthless. (It was, as Sherman put it, "as far from our future possible wants as was possible to discover.") Worthless or not, the Navajos chose to go home.

"If we are taken back to our own country," Barboncita told Sherman, "we will call you our father and mother. If there was only a single goat there, we would all live off of it."

Barboncita was a warrior, not an orator, but listen to his words:

"I hope to God you will not ask to go to any country but our own. When the Navajos were first created, four mountains and four rivers were pointed out to us, inside of which we should live, and that was to be Dinetah. Changing Woman gave us this land. Our God created it specially for us."

The tribe voted unanimously the next day to return to Dinetah. A reservation including part of the San Juan Valley and the Chuska and Carizzo mountains was drawn. It was far less than the Navajos had occupied before 1864 and included none of the four sacred mountains which hold their world together. But Barboncita was pleased.

"It is the very heart of our country," he said.

One of those four mountains is Mount Taylor. Manuelito recalled that when the Navajos topped the ridge west of the Rio Grande on their famous Long Walk home they saw its peak outlined against the western horizon. He said his men—hard-bitten survivors of three years of desperate, hopeless combat—wept for joy. This is Tso Dzil, the Turquoise Mountain. Here rests the head of the great Yei whose spirit-body circles across Mount Blanco in the Sangre de Cristos and Mount Hesperus in the La Platas to the San Francisco Peaks above Flagstaff, encircling the Dinetah with harmony. The Holy People built this mountain with earth brought from the Third World, decorated it with turquoise, blue cloud, and female rain, pinned it to earth with a magic stone knife, and left Tliish Tsoh (Bit Snake) to guard it. It was here the Hero Twins opened their campaign to make Dinetah safe for The People by killing the first of the monsters. (The blood of One Walking Giant forms the great lava flows across which Interstate 40 cuts a five-mile swath east of Grants.) And here Turquoise Girl lives, forever guarding the heart of Barboncita's country.

Much of this original Dinetah can be seen on an easy drive up N.M. 44 to the Farmington-Shiprock area, and then down U.S. 666 to Gallup, which is in fact as well as claim the Indian Capital of the United States. With a few appropriate side trips, this route will take you through the Holy Land of the Navajo religion. And if the light is right, the cloud formations suitably dramatic, the sunsets as flamboyant as usual, you may glimpse why the Navajos chose to keep this arid land Changing Woman gave to them, and why Alex Atcitty left a good job in Los Angeles to come home.

Navajos arrived in Dinetah not much later than A.D. 1000. They were hunters and seed gatherers. They spoke an Athapaskan language, as do their cousins, the Apaches, and many tribes of western Canada. (I'm told that Navajos who listened to a tape recording made of a Carrier Indian in Canada could understand nearly every word.) Anthropologists believe they drifted in from the north in small clan-groups. Navajo mythology is more specific.

The Holy People climbed into the Dinetah from an underworld, emerging from the flooding Third World through a hollow reed. These Holy People included First Man and First Woman and most of the insect, bird, and animal people. The exact point of emergence is as hard to locate as is the Garden of Eden. However, we know that First Man lived at Huerfano Mountain, and that he found the infant Changing Woman crying on top of Gobernador Knob, less than thirty miles away across the Rio Arriba County border. In this same area, Black God helped First Man and First Woman hang the stars in the sky. (Coyota, always mischievous, flipped the star-filled storage blanket and created the Milky Way.) It was near here that Changing Woman created the first human Navajos out of fragments of skin rubbed from her body. (Atcitty's clan, the Bitter Water, was formed from her right armpit.) And it was here that most of the great poetic curing and blessing ceremonials of The People seem to have taken form.

As you drive up N.M. 44 with Nageezi Trading Post behind and Bloomfield twenty-two miles ahead, you pass Huerfano Mountain on your right. As the Spanish name suggests (*huerfano* means "orphan," or "alone"), it's all by itself—a huge rectangular monolith of stone that rises to 7,470 feet out of the chamisa and creosote brush expanse of the Blanco plateau. The oil companies that lined the rim of this sacred mesa with seventeen radio-broadcasting towers have also built roads providing easy access to the spectacular scenery of Blanco Canyon. And just eight miles beyond Huerfano is the entry to the Angel Peak Recreation Area, where the sun slanting against several hundred million years of fantastic, multicolored erosion creates memorable beauty. The Holy People called this the Glittering World. Standing on an overlook at Angel Peak one sees why.

The northeastern landmark of Dinetah is Shiprock—reached through Farmington, the San Juan Valley, and the town of Shiprock. The town is a major administrative center for this part of the reservation and, as Huerfano represents the Navajo past, it represents the tribal future. Here is a miniboom of look-alike public housing, the pickup-crowded parking lots of Fairchild Semiconductor, the bustle of the oil and gas industry, the beginnings of a tourist industry. On the mesa above Fruitland to the east looms the controversial Four Corners Power Plant and feeding it is Navajo Coal Mine, already the world's largest and growing fast. Here soon will be the 110,000-acre Navajo Irrigation project, and here is where El Paso Natural is asking the Interior Department for permission to open a $400 million operation to convert coal into gas (40,000 acres with an estimated yield of 700 million tons of coal are under lease).

Whatever position you take on the air pollution controversy surrounding it, the power complex is worth seeing. The entry road climbs less than a mile out of the lush irrigation of Fruitland into a surreal world. The mine, tied to the plant with broad paved coal roads, beggars description. Its mountainous waste piles stretch ten miles—so incredibly huge that in a landscape of grotesque exaggerations they almost manage to look natural. The power plant, too, is vast enough to overpower a less dramatic setting. But behind it across the blue water of Morgan Lake loom the great mottled hump of Hogback Mountain and the cathedral spire of Shiprock twenty miles away—blue against a brewing snowstorm. The man-made plant is properly dwarfed.

From as far south as Grey Mountain, as far north as Colorado, and as far west as Yazzi in the Arizona Lukachukai Mountains, Shiprock juts like a great thumb into the sky. It's a strange formation, the plaster cast of the inside of a volcano. The volcano cone has been worn away by millions of years of wind and rain, leaving only the tough igneous rock which once bubbled and boiled in its throat. This core towers 1,450 vertical feet above the grassy plain—twenty stories taller than the Empire State Building.

Shiprock is hard to describe. One remembers how it looked the last time he saw it, and how it looked in the hundred photographs he has seen. But when he approaches it again—this time on a November afternoon with a snow squall sliding down the sky out of Utah—he finds that both memory and pictures have lied. Under the sun and against the blue desert sky Shiprock had provided a foreboding contrast—its ragged bulk suggesting the cataclysmic violence of its birth. But against this day's stormy, troubled cloudscape it soars timeless and serene—proof against the violence of the sky.

One way to reach it is via Navajo Route 13, which leaves U.S. 666 seven miles south of Shiprock town and ambles forty-five miles westward through Buffalo Pass. The Navajo gravel has long since vanished and the first half-mile is rough. But after that it's a pleasant drive. From the junction the angle of vision merges Rol-Hay Rock and Table Mesa (six miles south) into a single shape. It suggests the ultimate aircraft carrier, twenty stories tall and three miles long, anchored in a sea of gramma grass. Eight miles from 666 this road passes through a break in the most dramatic of those volcanic walls that radiate from Shiprock. I find this wall hard to believe.

The wall probably formed during the great Neogenic volcanic period, which thrust Mount Taylor 11,390 feet into the sky, caused the mind-boggling Valle Grande explosion, and scattered ashes from Utah to Kansas. The stone crust of the earth cracked open here. From the base of Shiprock volcano creeks radiate outward, miles long but only three or four feet wide. Red-hot plastic rock squeezed up through these cracks and through the heavy ash above like toothpaste from a tube. On this day, perhaps fifteen million years later, only a sloping buttress of earth remains of the ash. The great wall stands exposed.

It is snowing now on Beautiful Mountain ten miles to the

southwest and the breeze is gusty, cool, and damp. In places, holes have been eroded through the wall and through these holes the breeze funnels and becomes wind enough to set up a muted howling. The wall wanders almost due north toward Shiprock and from the buttress of earth the immensity of this monolith makes it seem only a few hundred yards away. It is almost four miles, and as one walks along it, alone, drafted, with the west wind playing it like a grotesque stone flute, it is easier to buy the Navajo view of man as part of nature than the whiteman's view of himself as master of it.

Shiprock is rarely visited. The old tracks following the wall are almost erased. Once one walks a few hundred yards from the road the only clue that others share this planet is the corpse of a car abandoned here years ago. West of the wall, a mile or so away, is the homestead of a Navajo family—small house, sheds, corrals, and hogan. The Navajo cooperates with the mystique of this place by using his grazing permit to raise horses. They range on the landscape below, a mixed bag of colors and types with enough pintos and paints included to satisfy a movie casting director.

In mythic times the Navajo would not have been safe here. Tse Ninahaleeh, the Winged Monster, nested in the cliffs of this Rock with Wings. Like other monsters inhabiting the Glittering World, it ate people. But somewhere north of Huerfano, Changing Woman had slept beside a waterfall, and had become pregnant, and had borne twin sons, and their names were Monster Slayer and Child Born of Water. Their father was the errant sun, and around these twins Navajo mythology has woven an Odyssey which rivals the tales of Homer.

Monster Slayer tricked Winged Monster into dropping him

into the monster's nest atop Shiprock. There he killed the beast. He persuaded the monster's offspring to foreswear monsterhood and become instead the eagle and the owl. And then he persuaded Spider Woman to rescue him from his impossible perch by lowering him in a basket.

Tribal mythology also credits Spider Woman with teaching the Navajos to weave—a craft which The People have made an art. And while the myths assign no particular home to this Holy Person a logical place would be Two Grey Hills, the site of the finest flowering of her teaching.

One reaches this old trading post by turning off U.S. 666 at Jewcomb Junction, thirty miles south of Shiprock. The dirt road goes twelve miles westward to the Toadlena boarding school in the Chuska Mountains. Halfway there, looking exactly the way a trading post should look, is Two Grey Hills. The road winds out of a wash and here to your right front are a barn with attached cattle and sheep pens and a long, low building with a single gasoline pump and a line of pickup trucks in front.

For one raised, as I was, at a rural crossroads, Two Grey Hills is undiluted nostalgia. Like the defunct general store, the trading post stocks everything—groceries, kerosene for the hogan stove, clothing, veterinary medicine, school supplies, sheep salt, graduation presents. And, like my father's store, this one is as much social center as shopping center. As a stranger where strangers are rare I represent a welcome diversion. The dozen men and women inside eye me with polite interest. Three men wearing the inevitable big hat-denims-mackinaw and boots uniform of cattle country discuss my cumbersome camera in Navajo. One is wearing a black sweatshirt emblazoned "Sigma Alpha Epsilon" over the legend "University of Michigan." This incongruity strikes me as funny and we catch ourselves—SAE and I—grinning at each other in friendly mutual amusement.

On this day Derald Stock's supply of rugs is down to a couple of dozen. The prices range from a low of sixty-five dollars to a high of nine hundred dollars. Each pattern is different, produced from a design which exists in the weaver's imagination. Each is formed from hand-carded natural wool—black, white, gray, and brown—untouched by dye. (In some parts of the reservation weavers use natural dyes, but not here.) Stock notes that two things are happening to the Navajo rug business. Since about 1967, prices have been soaring. The value has doubled for average rugs and increased 500 or 600 percent for the finer ones. And the art is dying out.

"I sold a really fine tapestry yesterday—a little smaller than three by five feet—to a collector for thirty-five hundred dollars," Stock said. "A really good weaver can make one like that with a year's work, and maybe two or three little ones. Out of that money you buy your own materials. It's demanding work for low pay and the young women just aren't bothering to learn it."

It is sundown when you leave Two Grey Hills and you drive down the Chuska Valley toward Gallup through the gathering darkness. To your right, a dot of yellow light appears at the base of Grey Mountain—one hogan in an infinity of night. With 120,000 people occupying over sixteen million acres, Navajo country has a population of less than one family per square mile. And yet for its farming-livestock economy, the reservation is terribly overcrowded. A million and a half acres are "wild lands," mesa and desert useless for grazing. Only 5 percent will support as much as forty sheep per square mile. Nearly half of the tribe's pastures require up to sixty-five acres to feed a single animal. Rainfall averages less than ten inches a year and, typical of desert climate, much of it arrives in quick, violent "male rain" storms. In the winter, blizzards kill cattle and sometimes The People as well. In the summer water is scarce. Materially, this Dinetah offers little. (As Atcitty once said, "Saying Rich Navajo is like saying Tiny Giant.")

But there are other things to remember. In the Emergence Myth, the name the Holy People put on evil was "The Way To Make Money." And the Hero Twins decided to spare the lives of the final monsters so The People would learn from living with them. Those monsters were named Fatigue, Old Age, Hunger, and Poverty. Poverty, one suspects, is as much a permanent resident of Dinetah as is enduring Shiprock. But there is also the stark, austere, everlasting beauty of the land.

In the Nightway ceremonial, the singer chants:

> In the house made of dawn,
> In the house made of sunset light
> In the house made of rain cloud
> With beauty before me, I walk
> With beauty behind me, I walk
> With beauty all around me, I walk.

If the landmarks of Dinetah have helped form the Navajo religion, it seems equally certain that its beauty has helped form the Navajo character.

The Mountain on the Guardrail at Exit 164B

Pause a moment on the bridge that carries Albuquerque's Louisiana Boulevard across Interstate Highway 40. Just below, the twice-a-day tide of rush-hour traffic clamors eastward. Behind you, vehicles escaping from the freeway via Exit 164B eject themselves into the crowded northbound lanes of the boulevard. Within the circle of your vision live a third of the citizens of New Mexico. This is the focus of its commerce, its traffic, its tension. This trembling bridge at 5:10 P.M. is as close as one can come in New Mexico to the nightmare of urban America.

On this particular autumn afternoon I drive through the exit with a Cadillac, frantic with hurry, just behind me. To my left a pickup wearing its dents like a boxer's scars signals a right turn into my path of escape. The Aspiring Age demands another of its endless sterile decisions. I might as well be in Chicago, or Newark, or Indianapolis, or Fort Worth.

It is exactly at this spot and at this moment that Mount Taylor comes into view. As you roll nervously into the acceleration lane, the Turquoise Mountain rises majestically over the guardrail. Today a convection layer has trapped Albuquerque's bad breath and filled the Rio Grande Valley with smog. Across this gray haze, the ancient volcano floats blue with distance and white with early snow.

When he built it as the home of Turquoise Girl, the First Man of Navajo mythology pinned it to the ground with a magic knife. But smog (or fog over Nine Mile Hill in the Rio Puerco breaks) causes the knife to slip and the mountain to hang halfway between earth and sky. Tomorrow, perhaps, it will be earthbound again, looking mountainlike and suggesting the serenity that mountains bring to mind. It is rarely the same on consecutive viewings—changing with the sun, the season, and the weather; sometimes a stark indigo outline against a garish sunset horizon, sometimes white, sometimes only a hazy, hinted mountain, sometimes wearing its clouds like a blowing scarf, sometimes piling them into stratospheric thunderheads.

You escape each afternoon from the world of Exit 164B, depleted by the day. If you look across the guardrail it is there, reminding you of a different world, of silence, and the smell of fir, and the possibility of wild turkey. My map tells me the Turquoise Mountain is 62.7 miles from this noisy intersection. In another sense the distance is infinite.

3

We All Fall Down

At the northern fringe of the village of Pecos, New Mexico, a ridgeline rises between the Pecos River and the narrow valley of Cow Creek. The ridge is cut by arroyos and covered with a mixed stand of piñon pine, juniper, and cedar. Amado Ortega often came here from his home at the edge of the village to hunt rabbits. Here, on the twenty-first or twenty-second of June, 1961, he shot and skinned a bobcat. This ridge was to be circled in black on the map and labeled Area I.

Fourteen miles east of this site, Area II was to be marked off on the slope of El Barro Peak, which rises to an altitude of more than eight thousand feet above Tecolote Canyon. The piñon grows taller here, since rainfall increases with elevation, and El Barro also bears a scattering of aspen, spruce, and ponderosa pine. Amado Ortega came here on or about June 19, and worked through the day felling timber for the sawmill that sometimes employed him. He may have noticed, as others did later, that cottontail rabbits, chipmunks, and other small rodents were unusually scarce on the mountain.

Four miles northeast of Pecos, Cow Creek is lined with yellow pine. Below the road, Cow Creek meadow is knee-deep in grass and spotted with bright blue patches of wild iris. Mr. Ortega came here to train a colt for his seven children to ride. While it is not possible to establish the exact date of his visit, a circle was marked around this serene little mountain pasture and it became Area III.

There is no doubt when Amado Ortega was in Area IV. The date was June 23. He came in the morning, driving a small flock of sheep to graze on the buffalo grass that grows on the low hill where the Pecos National Monument is located. This is the site of the Cicuye Indian Pueblo, deserted since the year before George Washington began his first term as president of the United States. The landscape here is dominated by the roofless ruins of the Church of Nuestra Señora de Los Angeles de Porciuncula. Its mud-mortared stone walls rise fifty feet above the dissolved adobe outlines of the old pueblo and brood over its own decayed *convento*. This historic site is surrounded by a barbed wire fence, but sheep are not respecters of wire. They may have wandered under the fence and Ortega may have followed them. Perhaps he ate his lunch in the deep shade of the roofless transept, since June is the hottest month of the high country summer and elsewhere in Area IV shade is scarce.

When one sits in this shade with the worn stone against his back and the past spread before him, it is easy—almost natural—to think of death. The massive old church is dead, and so is the ruined pueblo in the sunlight outside. Violent death was once familiar here. To the Cicuye people, it came almost every year from the great buffalo plains to the east in the form of Comanche raiding parties. To the Franciscan friars and monks, it came in 1680 in the form of a knotted calendar cord delivered by a Taos Indian runner. The cord told the Cicuye warrior clans that the date had been set for the Pueblos to rise against the Spanish. When the last knot was counted, the priests were slain here, where the wind now pushes the tumbleweeds across the abandoned floor.

But young men are less likely to think of death, and Amado Ortega was just thirty-eight, and in such robust health that he had never visited a doctor. Since he was a hunter, he may have noticed that there were no rabbits to be seen and that even the burrows of the tiny deer mice seemed deserted. But Amado Ortega would have had no reason to sense danger in the unusual silence. He may have wondered about that, but would have had no reason for nervousness even if he had happened to know that in 1837 the Indians who had inhabited Cicuye for a thousand years had sickened and died by the hundreds; that only seventeen had escaped alive from a pueblo which had counted its warriors in the hundreds and had housed seven secret societies, each with its own underground kiva.

It is quite likely that there was nothing dangerous in the vicinity of the Cicuye ruins when Ortega was there with his sheep. It seems probable that this young man had been fatally touched before June 23. It may have happened in one of the other three areas circled on the map, or perhaps Mr. Ortega had been many other places in the week of June 20. No one would guess how important it would be to know exactly where Amado Ortega had been until the second week in July. Then it would be too late to ask him.

Amado Ortega died the night of June 29 in St. Vincent Hospital at Santa Fe. He died in a peculiar fashion, leaving a puzzled medical staff and a chest X-ray described, with a vigor of language unusual in the medical profession, as "quite bizarre."

The story of his death, written while he was dying and in the hours before a postmortem examination was completed, reflects the bafflement of his doctors.

"This 38-year-old white male became very ill suddenly about five days ago. He noticed a feeling of a lump in the left chest. This hurt him to breathe, and hurt him to move his arms about. He tried to go back to work but felt ill and noticed pains in his knees. The day before yesterday he became very short of breath and was admitted to the hospital yesterday afternoon at which time he was started on Digitalis. Blood cultures were taken and he was placed in oxygen. He has been very well. He has worked in a sawmill and has used no sprays indoors. There is no history of diabetes in the family, or of tuberculosis."

An electrocardiogram had revealed nothing helpful. But the attending physician did notice, and record, an unusual symptom. "Even in oxygen, the nailbeds and lips were a dusky cyanotic color."

To be exact, they were the color of the Black Death. Had a physician of the fourteenth century seen these signs he would have evacuated the city. As those words were written on his chart Amado Ortega was dying of bubonic plague in its wildly infectious pneumonic form.

More than a week passed before pathologists pinned down

the cause of death. Cultures produced from samples of blood did not reveal the fatal microorganism. A culture was then made from tissue in Mr. Ortega's lungs. In this, a bacteriologist peering through a powerful microscope saw tiny bipolar rods—members of the plant kingdom called *Pasteurella pestis*. No organism has had more impact on the history of Western civilization. And none, with the possible exception of cholera, has killed more humans.

The Scandinavians personified bubonic plague as the goddess Hel, a hag who came with a broom and swept the countryside clean of life. Throughout the Middle Ages and into the Renaissance it rode as one of the Four Horsemen of the Apocalypse, as Pestilence, flanked by War, Death, and Famine. It was the subject of Brueghel's chilling masterpiece, *The Emperor*, and inspired many of Holbein's famous woodcuts. Pope Clement VI ordered a census of its victims after spice ships brought *Pasteurella pestis* to Genoa in 1348. A death toll of more than 42,800,000 was tallied in this survey, and historians estimate that the population of Europe was reduced a third by this five-year pandemic. The toll included an estimated 90 percent of the citizens of London and all but five of the residents of Smolensk. It was to flare up again, and again, and again for five centuries—blamed on comets, on vapors, and on sin. It was to close Shakespeare's theater, kill Titian and Petrarch's Laura and Boccaccio's father, and provide the subject of literature's grimmest reportage in Daniel Defoe's *Journal of the Plague Year*.

This same deadly pestilence was now abroad in the northern New Mexico high country, and the news of it went immediately to a young man named Bryan E. Miller. Somewhere in a vast expanse of forests and mountains Amado Ortega had come in contact with a "foci" of *Pasteurella pestis*. As chief of the Vector Control Service of the New Mexico Department of Public Health it was Miller's job to find this spot of infection and prevent its spread.

To Miller, the plague was an old and familiar adversary. A World War II Navy veteran, he had taken a degree in wildlife biology at the University of Wyoming and had done graduate work there and at the University of California. His education had made him a biologist, his profession had made him a hunter, and circumstance had decreed that his quarry would often be *Pastuerella pestis* and the animals and insects through which it is transmitted to humans.

Bubonic plague was first detected in New Mexico in 1938 when it caused a die-off of prairie rodents. The first human case went into the records in 1949, quickly followed by four others. Miller, then a field man for the U.S. Public Health Service, was sent to the state in 1950 and spent two years checking known plague "foci" points and searching for new ones. He found such spots of infection in twenty-two of the thirty-two New Mexico counties.

The plague had then ebbed in New Mexico, as it has done in its mysterious fashion down through recorded history. Isolated cases cropped up in California, Oregon, Idaho, Nevada, and Utah, but in New Mexico *Pasteurella pestis* seemed dormant until 1959. Then a twelve-year-old girl living at Sandia Park in the mountains above Albuquerque was stricken with the plague and died en route to a hospital. The following year, two airmen stationed at Roswell Air Force Base went rabbit hunting and found the Black Death instead. Good luck, instant diagnosis, and antibiotic drugs saved both men. In each case, Miller had been able to exactly trace the whereabouts of the victims during the period of potential infection. This made the task of finding the source of the bacilli relatively simple. The name of Amado Ortega's home village was enough to tell Miller he would badly need this sort of luck again.

Even if the biologist had not been aware of the dreadful history of the plague, the site of the latest case and the season of the year combined to lend urgency to the hunt. Pecos, a village of six hundred people, is built at the mouth of Pecos Canyon, the most popular gateway to the Pecos Wilderness Area. Upstream are hundreds of thousands of acres of mountains, forests, lakes, and trout streams. Uncounted thousands of fishermen, campers, and picknickers funnel through the village each summer. Only six miles away to the west is the Glorieta Baptist Assembly, which draws more thousands of summer visitors from throughout the South and West for religious training sessions. If an epizootic of plague was causing a rodent die-off in an area exposed to these visitors and their families the effects could be disastrous. Children love to chase chipmunks, golden mantle squirrels, and other small mountain animals. Sick animals are easily caught, and they would be captured at the time when the fleas they carry were loaded with plague bacilli.

Exactly this had happened in one of the earlier cases. A child had caught a dying prairie dog near the village of Glorieta and had been fatally infected by a fleabite. If the children of tourists were so infected, they would likely be scattered at their homes across the land before the usual two-to-five-day incubation period of *Pasteurella pestis* ended and the first symptoms of the disease appeared. They would probably not be seen by northern New Mexico doctors, now alert to the presence of the plague. It is unlikely that a doctor who has not been alerted, and who has neither seen nor heard of a plague case in his entire career, will guess right when he sees its early symptoms. They resemble those of a multitude of common ailments. But if a second guess is required, it is probably too late. *Pasteurella pestis* multiplies by division of its single cell into two parts, doubling its number each twenty minutes. At this rate, one rod becomes 68 billion rods in twelve hours. As these rods die, they produce a toxin which destroys the walls of blood vessels. Thus, in its later stages treatment which destroys the bacilli subjects the patient to a massive flood of its poisonous toxin.

Miller dropped a mosquito control project on which he was working, loaded seventy-five traps into his car, and hurried to Pecos with Eddie Rodriguez, a health sanitarian.

"Before you can trap," says Miller, "you have to talk." Since the man who could have told them everything was dead, the two interviewed his widow, the parish priest, friends, co-workers, everyone who might have some knowledge which would help retrace Ortega's movements of the week before his illness. From this pattern of questions, patiently repeated, the shape of Amado Ortega and his way of life began to emerge. He was a reticent man who often rose early, saddled his horse, and rode away, telling no one where he was going and never mentioning where he had been. When jobs could be found he took them, cutting timber for the sawmill or herding sheep for neighbors. When there were no jobs, he hunted in the mountains, returning at night with small game for the pot or fur pelts for the market.

While the questioning continued in the village, at the lumber camps, and at the mountain cabins, Miller's traps were collecting samples of wildlife on the hillsides and canyons around the Ortega home. Examination of the animals taken told nothing, except that the animals were healthy. The answers to the questions told little more—only enough for Miller to mark out four areas where Ortega was known to have been. Day-long gaps left in the map of the victim's movements meant he might have been infected almost anywhere in the vast territory which New Mexicans call the Pecos country. If Miller was lucky he would find the plague foci in one of the four areas. If he wasn't he would find it only by careful, methodical, process-of-elimination trapping of the entire district.

Miller set out his trap lines first in the two areas where Ortega's movements were best established—on El Barro and around the Cicuye ruins. He worked, as plague hunters always do, against time and the knowledge that the bacilli might even now be spreading in a chain reaction. This had happened in San Francisco in 1900, killing 113 of the 121 persons infected. It had happened again in Oakland, California, in 1919, when a victim, infected with pneumonic plague by a squirrel flea, spread the bacilli with his cough before he died.

When you talk to Miller you notice instantly that his eyes are blue, because they contrast so vividly with a face burned a deep and permanent brown by years of sun and wind. When you watch him work, you notice that his eyes are trained, seeing the tiniest track of the mountain rodents and missing none of the almost invisible signs which animal life leaves behind it. Now Miller was hunting traces of death, as well as life, because the broom of the Black Death still sometimes sweeps as clean as it did in medieval Scandinavia. He was finding almost nothing. There were none of the shriveled remains the plague would have left. Diligent trapping produced only eleven live rodents around the ruins, and a few more on El Barro. These seemed healthy, and laboratory examination proved them plague-free.

While Miller and an assistant were narrowing their hunt, a thirty-eight-year-old research geologist named Dr. Robert Johnson was boarding an airliner at Santa Fe Municipal Airport for a return flight to his home in Massachusetts. On the web of skin between the thumb and first finger of his left hand he had noticed a tiny sore spot, the sort of sore Dr. Johnson might have shrugged off, with terrible irony, as just a fleabite.

Had Dr. Johnson delayed his departure long enough for the inevitable fever to develop he might have been saved. Santa Fe doctors at the moment were extremely plague-conscious. Massachusetts had never in history had reason to be.

At his home near Boston, Dr. Johnson began suffering from a headache. He complained of nausea and a physician called to examine him found his fever was 102 degrees. The next morning he felt better, but by night his lungs were failing and he began coughing blood. An ambulance rushed him to a hospital. There his blood pressure dropped dramatically and he lost consciousness. X-rays showed the same bizarre wreckage of lungs that had puzzled Amado Ortega's doctors. Death was quick.

The news that the plague had killed its second victim was disturbing enough to Miller. What disturbed him more was the information which accompanied the news. Dr. Johnson had been working on an erosion research project just a few miles west of Santa Fe. Miller knew the city was currently infested with colonies of prairie dogs, a rodent terribly susceptible to *Pasteurella pestis*. A few years earlier biologists in Colorado had estimated a million of these animals wiped out when an epizootic of plague swept through their colonies in the Middle Park country. This summer, prairie dogs were at the peak of one of their cycles of population explosion. Their towns thrived in the field adjoining Santa Fe's Second Street, beside the Little League baseball diamond in Ashbaugh Park, and all around the city. They had invaded lawns and garages in the Casa Alegre residential district, had been run over by cars and captured by children. If the bacilli which had killed Dr. Johnson reached the colonies of these animals west of the city, the disease would spread certainly and rapidly into the residential districts.

Miller suspended his hunt in the Pecos country and hurried to Santa Fe—eighteen miles over the Sangre de Cristo mountain ridge to the northwest. Here he was joined by important reinforcements. Frank Prince, chief of the San Francisco Field Station of the U.S. Public Health Service and a veteran plague hunter, arrived by plane. With him came Dr. Bruce Hudson and biologist Al Kinney, both Health Service plague experts.

The team moved to a deserted ranch headquarters which Dr. Johnson had used as a base camp while studying the movement of soil particles in eroding arroyos. They found three empty residences, a Navajo-type hogan barn and corral, two outdoor toilets, and a storage shed. There were signs that Johnson had lived in one of the houses and evidence that rodents ranged in all of the buildings. The dried remains of several deer mice were found in one building, apparently dead for several months. Miller also found a large amount of bleached rabbit droppings and other signs that cottontails had been plentiful in the area the previous summer. Now neither rabbits, nor tracks, nor fresh pellets were to be found. Something had wiped out the rabbit population, and Miller knew rabbits are likely victims of *Pasteurella pestis.*

But as the search continued, hope that the source of the plague could be isolated here began to fade. Bones of last year's rabbits were found where they had been dragged into the nests of wood rats. Yet when the plague strikes, wood rats are normally the first to die. The fact that they were still plentiful—and in robust health—indicated a different disease had killed the rabbits. This conclusion was reinforced when Miller and Prince found that the area's kangaroo rats had been wiped out with the cottontails. This long-tailed rodent is resistant to bubonic plague.

While the traps were doing their work, interrogation of friends of the geologist turned up some interesting information. One remembered that Johnson had mentioned making a trip into the Pecos Wilderness Area. He might have entered this trackless 165,000-acre expanse from its Peñasco Valley back door. But he was equally likely to have gone through the village of Pecos.

Miller and his associates turned their attention back to the Pecos country. The ranch and its environs were circled on the map, labeled Area V, and left for more intensive investigation later. Before plague hunters could return, there would be an Area VI, but it would be miles away.

In the Pecos country, a detachment from Walter Reed Hospital joined the hunt. A makeshift laboratory was set up at the Pecos Fish Hatchery two miles upstream from the village to make preliminary examinations of the animals being snared in the spreading network of traps. The rainy season was now in full force in the high country, causing complications. By the end of June, thunderheads begin piling above the mountain peaks. At first they produce only the rumble of thunder, a bombardment of lightning, and the state's annual forest fire season. But in late July and August, the clouds tower high into the stratosphere, form caps of ice crystals, and deluge the high slopes with torrential rain and hail. The rain made the back trails impassable for vehicles, swept away animal signs, and made trapping difficult. The plague team was ready for a change in luck.

This came on the afternoon of August 5. The telephone rang in the Pecos office of Dr. Leslie M. FitzGerald, the only physician serving the mountain country. Arnold Benson, president of the Pecos Power and Light Company, was calling from Cowles on the border of the Pecos Wilderness Area to report that one of his construction workers had suddenly become ill. The worker, Ignacio Padilla, was being rushed to the doctor's office—a distance of some twenty miles via the road which winds out of the mountains down Pecos Canyon.

Dr. FitzGerald said in a subsequent report that "in view of the two previous plague cases in the past month in this same area, the thought of bubonic plague seemed to keep entering my mind even before the arrival of the patient." When Padilla was brought in at 5:15 P.M., Dr. FitzGerald immediately looked for plague symptoms and immediately found them. On each side of the patient's groin typical examples of plague "bubos" had formed, already hard and discolored and the size of small walnuts. In the time of Oliver Cromwell, a physician brave enough to approach such a sufferer would have attempted to burn off these bubos with a hot iron. Dr. FitzGerald instead gave Mr. Padilla a massive gram-and-a-half shot of streptomycin and four grams of sulfadiazine. He continued the treatment with these two drugs for forty-eight hours. By then, Mr. Padilla's fever had subsided, the swellings had disappeared, and laboratory examination of blood samples had disclosed that Dr. FitzGerald had guessed right and saved a life.

Dr. FitzGerald's fast action had also given the plague hunters their first break—a man who had been touched by *Pasteurella pestis* and was still alive to talk about it. Miller and his associates cross-examined Padilla. Exactly where had he been every hour of the past several days? He had been only at home and at work on Grass Mountain. Had he been bitten by any fleas? Not that he remembered. Had he seen any sick animals? No, but he remembered seeing two dead rodents of some sort. In fact, he had picked them up and dropped them in a hole dug for the base of a power line pole. They were now buried under the pole. Exactly where was this pole located? An X went on the map at the site. Here trapping operations would be immediately concentrated. The X was in easy range of Amado Ortega's horseback hunting trips. Dr. Johnson's path into the Pecos Wilderness Area might also have crossed it.

Grass Mountain rises to two miles above sea level in a massive ascending ridge between th canyons of Rio Valdez and the Pecos River. From the mountain, which takes its name from the broad meadows where elk herds feed, one can see open country only down the Pecos Valley to the south. In all other directions are timbered mountains. Its only vehicle access is a jeep trail which dead-ends at the boundary of the wilderness area. Along this trail are summer cabins, and the cabins were filled with vacationing couples and their children. Above the trail, Ignacio Padilla had been erecting utility poles. Miller and Prince set up a field laboratory here. They laid out their network of traps along animal runs, prayed that the thunderstorms building over the peaks around them would drift the other way, and combed the high meadows for the clues that *Pasteurella pestis* leaves—the bodies of its victims. They found almost nothing; only a deer mouse which proved to have died of an injury and a wisp of hair which might have been the remains of a predator's meal.

The rains kept their distance and the traps produced chipmunks, shrews, wood rats, whitefooted mice, deer mice, voles, and golden mantle squirrels. All were infested with fleas, but all were apparently healthy. The traps also attracted a black bear with an appetite for the rodents they contained. Bears are apparently plague resistant. Miller decided to shoot the animal and check his blood for antibodies which might tell if he had been eating infected animals. The bear disappeared.

The biologists performed field autopsies on the rodents they caught, saving fleas, spleens, and blood samples and carefully recording the site where each was snared. If laboratory results were negative, each animal processed would at least slightly narrow the circle of the hunt, telling not where the plague was, but where it wasn't. The monotonous work continued, and as it continued, the fear grew that Miller's X on the map merely marked a bad guess, that the plague which struck Padilla and Ortega had struck elsewhere and might, by now, be striking others.

Then Miller removed the spleen from a golden mantle squirrel and saw on this tiny organ an irregular pattern of dark spots, the sort of darkening which might be caused by the destruction of the walls of blood vessels. Tularemia might produce such spotting. So might other diseases. The toxin of the bacilli of the Black Death certainly would, for these dark splotches on the skin of dying men were the trademark which gave it its popular name. Miller suspected that the Pecos country foci of bubonic plague had been found.

More than seventy additional ground squirrels were caught while laboratory personnel tested culture produced from the spleen. Most of these, too, had this telltale spotting on internal organs. Word came back quickly from the laboratory. Culture injection into laboratory mice had killed the mice overnight. The mice had died of bubonic plague. There was no doubt now that the Grass Mountain ground squirrel clan was the host of the Black Death.

The plague team's task now involved continued trapping to wipe out the infected population and the planting of baited DDT dusting boxes across the mountainside to eliminate the fleas and break the infection cycle in the event diseased animals were missed. But the X remained on Miller's plague map, marking now a spot of suspicion to be routinely inspected year after year.

Trapping continued in all other areas and throughout the Pecos country, with no other traces of *Pasteurella pestis* found. But west of Santa Fe, the plague hunters found colored rocks in the arroyo bottom where Dr. Johnson had worked. They learned he used these paint-coded gravels to trace erosion movement in flash floods. The trappers used the same stones to trace Dr. Johnson, and finally found an infected family of whitefooted mice, a family to be wiped out and an area to be decontaminated and watched.

The rainy season had ended now and the immense calm of autumn settled over the mountains. The aspens turned yellow on the high slopes and the snow came, ending trapping and sending the tiny rodents which die of bubonic plague, and sometimes carry it dormant in their bodies, into the winter-long sleep of hibernation.

When summer came again, the plague seemed to have vanished from the Sangre de Cristo Mountains as mysteriously as it had come. The *New England Journal of Medicine* published a technical report on the 1961 outbreak, reporting that bacilli of the Black Death had been found in fifteen western states and reminding physicians that bubonic plague "is still present, still as virulent as ever, and a threat with grave implications if it bursts its bounds." The year passed quietly, but when 1963 came a Navajo shepherd shot a rabbit in Arizona, and fed it to his sheep dogs, and died five days later of bubonic plague in a hospital at Gallup—two hundred miles west of the Sangre de Cristo Mountains. In Colorado, *Pasteurella pestis* was found in animals on a Lowry Field bombing range. In New Mexico, and throughout the West, Miller and men of his profession watched the old plague foci and hunted new ones, knowing it will continue its odd cycle of killing until science finally finds a way to erase it from the countryside.

And in the schoolyard at Pecos, and elsewhere where the younger children play the older games, the voices at recess still sing "Ring around the Rosy" almost as the children sang it in the Middle Ages, when the game was new.

The words in the fourteenth century were only a little different.

> *Ring around the roses,*
> *Pockets full of posies,*
> *Ka-Choo! Ka-Choo!*
> *We all fall down.*

Today the children do not know that a ring of rosemary blossoms and a pocket full of the aromatic petals was another of the desperate, hopeless prescriptions for warding off the Black Death. Now they substitute the words "Ashes, Ashes" for the bloody cough of pneumonic plague in the third line, and the macabre cynicism is missing when they sing, "We all fall down."

But the Black Death is still in the mountains.

The Messenger Birds

It is sleepy at Zuni Pueblo on the second day of Shalako. The dancing has lasted all night and most of the people here today haven't been to bed for thirty-six hours. Now it is early afternoon—a cold, still December day. The sun filters through a gauze of stratospheric ice crystals. The shadows are blue on the cliffs of Corn Mountain. Far to the east woodsmoke rises in front of Zuni Ridge without enough wind to smudge it. My back is braced against the corner post of one of the sheep pens that line the north side of Zuni River. My legs are stretched in front of me, their topsides warm from the sun, their backsides clammy from the frozen earth. The river carries only its winter trickle. Across it is the Holy Ground, fenced on three sides now by Zuni residences, where the Zuni clans made their last camp on their mythic search for the Middle Place of the World. In that clearing now, the six Shalako are dancing their annual farewell to their people. When they are finished, these messenger birds will return to Kothluwalawa, the Dance Hall of the Dead. The great masks which represent them will be returned to their secret places. Shalako will be over for another year.

I have no need now to watch the Shalako dance. I have come because I am working on a novel, the climax of which takes place in Zuni Village on the night of Shalako. I have come with a friend to collect some odds and ends of reality to make this fiction seem more true. I have found what I need. Indeed, my drowsy head is full of it.

What will I use? The smell of dust, the smell of butchered sheep, the smell of woodsmoke and human sweat. The hundreds of vehicles jammed along the margins of State Road 53. The two Navajo cowboys, brothers, wearing good silver and worn-out boots, full of whiskey, youth, and high spirits, playfully needling a young hippie who is also wearing a headband, beads, and silver and who, until the teasing began, had been absorbing Indian vibrations. The multiple tinkle of bells on ceremonial ankles, mixing with the tapping of ceramic drums and the piping of flutes. The sudden emergence down an unlit street of the Mudheads, their knobby incest-masks grotesque in the brief flash of a car's headlights. The thin chest of the Little Fire God slick with sweat as he dances. Which ones? What does it take to persuade a reader that you are showing him Zuni on a Shalako midnight? Will it be Saiyatasha, the Rain God of the North, standing on the roof of Longhorn House in the darkness singing his rhythmic Night Chant; or the boys with the basketball, dribbling, shooting baskets in their backyard, oblivious of the Council of the Gods coming down Greasy Hill behind them; or the young man wearing the University of New Mexico jacket, his face reverent, sprinkling cornmeal on the procession of kachinas passing him?

*   *   *

Across the river the Shalako swoop and dip in the odd dance that the Zunis call the race. They are planting feathered prayer plumes in holes in the holy ground. In the foreground, nearer the river, the Salamobia dance, the bristling turkey feather muffs and horizontal plumes giving their masks a fierceness. The crowd is thinner now and silent. From across the river comes the clacking sound of the Shalako's wooden beaks and the hooting of their voices. The pace of the Salamobia quickens. My friend lives at Black Rock and knows Zuni much better than I. He has told me that the Salamobia whose body and mask are colored black is a member of the Hekiapawa kiva. His totem is the mole, his direction is downward toward the Nadir of the earth, his color is darkness. The other Salamobia is a member of the Upanawa kiva, his mask is streaked with the many hues of the sky, his clan and his totem are the eagle. He dances now with a half-running gait, his yucca wands and his dance kilt shaking, the bells on his ankles faintly audible across the river.

"Take a look up," my friend says.

A halo has formed around the sun, a striking sight.

"I've seen them before," I said. "It's the sunlight refracting through frozen moisture in the stratosphere."

"I don't mean the halo," my friend said. "Can you see the eagles? Look just outside the halo, about seven o'clock."

There are two of them, almost too high to be visible. The sunlight glints through feathers, making them seem white. They swing in two intersecting circles almost directly over the dance ground.

"Male and female," says my friend, who benefits from better

eyes than mine, and more knowledge of golden eagles. "They hunt that way, I think."

I have heard of eagle eyes but it seems to me they are too high for hunting, and I saw so. If I can barely see them, big as they are, how can they see a tiny rodent in the grass?

"Okay, then," my friend says. "Let's say the Upanawa kiva has sent up its eagle fetish. Anyway, having them up there is something you can use in that novel."

But you can't. Fiction demands creditability.

4

The Conversion
of Cletus Xywanda

Biographers of Santa Fe, with the notable exception of
the late Oliver La Farge, have been inclined to talk of her in terms
of externals. They describe narrow, aimless streets; the softness
of adobe buildings, lilacs, and the long, red sunsets which flood
the cranky old city with gaudy colors. All this is there. The City
of the Holy Faith has been growing in its spectacular and im-
practical mountain setting since 1610 and its shows both its age
and its Spanish-Colonial origins. But the real essence of Santa Fe
is invisible and can't be communicated through adjectives. It has
something to do with the best of the women's clubs formally
naming itself "The Stitch and Bitch," something to do with the
good-natured insolence of plaza shoeshine boys, and something
to do with the cynical civic attitude toward growth and progress—
which Santa Feans view with no more enthusiasm than a milking

goat has for cold hands. It has something to do with lethargy and with tolerance (symptoms, perhaps, of old age). Most of all, it has something to do with people.

Therefore, I will turn to Cletus Cyprian Xywanda, who had a clear eye for people and highly unusual qualifications for judging the city. He also had a way with words. Ask a Santa Fean why he calls his town "The City Different" and the answer requires several thousand words (half pride, half irritation). Xywanda managed to sum up this differenmess in a single terse sentence. But to appreciate the aptness of his words, one needs to know something of the man and the circumstances.

Xywanda is a member of the Ibibio tribes, a citizen of Nigeria. He was then a subeditor of the Lagos *Morning Defender*—a periodical of considerable political clout in the coastal (Biafran) section of his African homeland. He came to Santa Fe one cold October Saturday under the sponsorship of the U.S. Information Agency to work as a guest observer-reporter on *The New Mexican*.

With this "emerging nation" background, Mr. Xywanda was not a man to be charmed—as American visitors usually are—by Santa Fe's surface features. No one had explained to him that Santa Fe is quaint (that useful adjective which covers so many civic sins). There was no appeal for him in the city's baffling labyrinth street system, or its mud buildings, or its appearance of having sprung from the earth—like fungus—innocent of foresight. After all, Lagos streets have mudholes equally deep, and buildings (in less attractive parts of the city) equally ramshackle, and it had developed with the same disdain of urban planning. When told by a proud local matron that Canyon Road, Santa Fe's most artsy and illogical thoroughfare, had originally been a foot-path used by Indians, Xywanda replied that Ogbomosh (the town of his nativity) had the same sort of problem but, with the help of a surveying crew and a bulldozer, was correcting it. In a word, Xywanda's first impression of "The City Different" was resound-ingly negative.

It was worsened by two factors. First, Xywanda had come to Santa Fe via New York—where he had spent several days sight-seeing. He had been impressed by Manhattan, which, as he put it, "glittered and roared," and he made endless comparisons be-tween Mayor Lindsey's Fun City and Santa Fe. Second, there was the bear affair.

As luck had it, a Santa Fe National Forest bear had picked the eve of Xywanda's arrival for a pre-hibernation garbage can raid. The bear had dawdled past the dawn. He had been spotted by some little girls en route to Acequia Madre grade school, who chased the beast into a garage and shut the door behind him. The city editor sent Xywanda along with a reporter-photographer to witness the efforts of the Game Department to evict the animal from the city limits.

Had Xywanda been from London, Paris, or Rome this episode might have amused him. But Xywanda was from the fringes of the Niger Basin rain forests. Wild animals in towns are also a problem in Nigeria, but the better towns are bringing it un-der control. The bear-in-the-garage reinforced Xywanda's suspi-cion that Santa Fe lacked sophistication. Before his visit was over, there were other incidents. A housewife opened a closet door and was set upon by a raccoon which had been inadvertently im-prisoned. A nearsighted visitor from Cleveland, baby-sitting with her grandchildren one night, assaulted a dog with a broom after it turned over a garbage can. To her amazement the dog scrambled up a backyard elm. Her son-in-law sought to settle her nerves by explaining that the animal she had attacked was not a dog, which can't climb trees even in Santa Fe, but a bear, but she flew back to Cleveland the next day. And that fall prairie dog colonies moved into the St. Michael's College athletic field, into a city park, and into Casa Alegre residential area. A college sprinter stepped into a prairie dog hole which had appeared overnight in the track and was disabled for the season. This caused the track coach to set out poison, which brought a local matriarch who likes animals to the scene with a pistol, which—according to police reports—she fired into the ground until her ammunition was exhausted. This seems to have frightened away both the coach and the prairie dogs, since nothing more was heard of the incident. But back to Xywanda.

It was traditional in those days that about midnight Saturday when the Sunday newspaper was coming off the press, the newsroom crew would retire to Frank's Lounge to celebrate the completion of the week. Mr. Xywanda joined the group, but not the celebration. He sat silently on his barstool, his cheetah-skin fez pulled low on his forehead and his expression morose. Finally he posed a question.

Why, he wondered, had the U.S. Department of State elected to send him to Santa Fe? While he hoped no offense would be taken from his remarks, it did seem odd, he said, that he, a subeditor of the *Morning Defender,* was sent to such a small community to observe the American press and American society. Why had not the State Department left him in New York? That city seemed well supplied with larger newspapers and seemed, in the regrettably short time he was allowed there, a metropolis of great interest.

While Mr. Xywanda phrased these questions politely, it developed that he suspected his trip from New York to New Mexico had been a trip into exile and reflected an official lack of respect on the part of the United States of America for the Republic of Nigeria. He sought reassurance. Instead (Frank's Lounge being what it was) he produced an argument.

Frank's Lounge, it should be noted here, was in those days a watering place favored by a social set called "the sweatshirt crowd." It occupied an ancient and dingy adobe on Palace Avenue a short block from Burro Alley. Some months after the evening here described, its entire west wall collapsed in a cloud of red dust, crushing the furnishings under tons of adobe blocks and tar-paper roofing—happily while the premises were vacant. Had the wall fallen on Saturday night, the City of the Holy Faith would have lost the flower of its manhood and most of its journalists as well. Frank and his crew moved next door into the new Palace Bar following the collapse, but his old clientele was never at ease amid the rococco comforts and cleanliness offered here, the new place soon became infested with lawyers, and the old debating society dispersed.

But on the night in question, Xywanda's remark stimulated a notable debate. Some agreed that New York was, in fact, more impressive than Santa Fe and that Xywanda had cause for disgruntlement. Another faction defended Santa Fe. The former noted that New York is larger and considerably taller (if memory serves, the point was made that only two Santa Fe buildings were high enough to offer the disconsolate any hope for a successful suicide leap) and much more lively. The latter countered that while the Empire State Building was indeed ninety-eight stories taller than the Bokum Building, the view from the top of the Bokum was longer—because one atop the Empire was lucky if he could see, through the smog, the traffic jam at Macy's directly below. The former argued that the city hadn't managed in 350 years to rid itself of prairie dogs, and hadn't managed to secure railroad service even from the railroad which bears its name, and tended to misspell the names of streets on official signs, and was probably the largest city this side of New Guinea which still drinks unfiltered lake water—its citizenry consoled by the hope that the algae which turns tap water green in the summer may contain vitamins.

The argument raged until the 2:00 A.M. closing time and covered a multitude of points of difference. New York is younger and looks to the sea. Santa Fe is old and looks to the mountains. New York's voice is the busy roar of the traffic. Santa Fe hears the wind in the cottonwoods and the bells of St. Catherine's Indian school. Even the birds were drawn into it (Santa Fe being overrun by birdwatchers). It was said that New York pigeons live nervously under the shadow of the falcons which roost in the cliffs of the city while Santa Fe pigeons lead sedentary lives protected by its squadrons of hawk-hating ravens. Xywanda listened alertly to all of this—his discontent turned to curiosity. No consensus was ever reached. Xywanda was left to find his own answer. And he did.

Six Saturdays later, Mr. Xywanda sat in the same bar. He had exchanged his work-a-day fez for a more formal camel-skin model, since this was to be his going-away party.

It developed as parties tended to develop at Frank's. Mr. Xywanda proposed a toast to Free Nigeria, the city editor offered a drink to the Confusion of the Boers, Xywanda raised a glass to Jomo Kenyatta, the police reporter drank to the fertility of Ibo cattle. And so it went until, finally, Xywanda declared that all present should drain a glass—at his expense—to Santa Fe.

He knew now, he told us, why the Department of State had sent him to our city. He would tell us, but first he wanted us to know how he had reached his conclusion. He had noticed, he said, that drivers sometimes traveled north on Cienega Street, although the signs indicate it is a one-way thoroughfare for southbound traffic only. He had remembered that in New York all drivers had moved in the same direction on one-way streets and he had been told those doing otherwise would be dealt with severely. He had asked about this Santa Fe custom and had learned that here the driver is expected to proceed in the direction indicated by the arrow unless he believes his reason for doing otherwise is sufficient to risk being caught and scolded by the police. The danger of a head-on collision, he was told, was slight since motorists here enter one-way streets with full knowledge that they may meet a noncomformist.

And then, Mr. Xywanda continued, there was the matter of his tribal robes. In New York, these had drawn attention, and some rude questioning about his place of origin.

"But in Santa Fe, people give me these." Mr. Xywanda reached under his white, red, yellow, green, and magenta robe into the breast pocket of his business suit, extracted a collection of political campaign cards, and fanned them on the table. They solicited his vote for the Republican nominees for sheriff, county clerk, land commissioner, and governor and the Democratic candidates for eleven offices at stake in the forthcoming November elections. "They think I am a citizen," Mr. Xywanda said. "They see my robes but they think I am a Santa Fean." Mr. Xywanda looked at us to assure himself that we understood the implications of this. A less courteous man might have noted that Santa Feans are sometimes eccentric in their dress.

"There is also the man who pretends to be a policeman," Xywanda said. He referred to an elderly citizen who had purchased a police cap and whistle and who, when the weather was mild, sometimes directed traffic on the plaza. Santa Feans were aware that this status was unofficial and since the whistle tooting and arm waving caused confusion only among tourists, the hobby was considered harmless.

"In New York," Xywanda said, "I think they would not let that man act like a policeman." He waited the polite moment for any sign of disagreement, received none, and went on.

"Tomorrow I go back to New York and I see the people around me all with three buttons on the front of the coat and the middle button buttoned, and all walking on the proper side of the sidewalk and waiting when the street signal says wait and not smoking when the sign is prohibitive and I will say to the man at the U.S. Information Agency there that in New York society transcends and the man is submerged within it. But Santa Fe . . ." Here Xywanda paused, with the talent of the natural-born talker, for the moment of suspense to underline his point.

"But Santa Fe celebrates the individual."

And that is exactly it. Santa Fe celebrates the individual.

The Apache Who Wouldn't Be Missed

The storekeeper was filling out a reservation fishing permit for me when this Jicarilla came in and stood there by the office door with his wife standing behind him. He was short and heavy-set with a band of blue cloth around his forehead and his hair in braids, and he just stood there patiently, waiting his turn. And finally the storekeeper looked up and he said, George, what can I do for you? And the Indian said, loan me a dollar. And the storekeeper said George, if I loan you a dollar you'll go right over to Gobernador and buy a jug of wine and that'll get you started and then your government check comes in tomorrow and instead of coming in to pay me what you already owe me, you'll stay over there at Gobernador and get drunk.

The Indian didn't say anything for a second until he was sure the storekeeper had finished talking and then he said loan me fifty cents. And the storekeeper said Damn it, George, do you remember where you were the last time I saw you? You were passed out in the ditch there west of Dulce and I took you into the hospital and that doctor there told you what this drinking was doing to you. If you get drunk like that again it's going to kill you.

And there was a moment of silence again and then the Indian said would you miss me?

The storekeeper just reached in his box there and handed George a dollar and he was laughing so hard he could hardly write it down in his notebook. But all he said was I'm sure glad I wasn't in the cavalry when we was fighting these Apaches.

5

The Hunt for the Lost American

The man had first appeared on this lonely ridge several days earlier. He had been on foot then, a tall, lanky, sunburned individual, moving slowly across the slopes of the Llano de Albuquerque—the great, empty landmass that rises between the Rio Grande and the Rio Puerco in north-central New Mexico. He paused at the wind erosion blowouts, examining the exposed stones. He spent hours along the banks of the shallow arroyos where gravel had been laid bare. He squatted at anthills, scrutinizing the tiny chips of flint the red fire ants bring to the surface from their tunnels. Some of these chips he sifted into an envelope before he left.

When he reappeared on the ridge in a pickup truck, he brought with him food and water, a wheelbarrow, a shovel, and wooden sifter frame bottomed with a quarter-inch mesh of wire.

Not far from the hills of the fire ants he began to dig, sampling a spot and then moving on. He dug carefully, lifting the loose topsoil from a compact layer of reddish earth beneath it, sifting it through the screen with a trowel, studying the stony residue, and making an occasional penciled note.

On the second day he found exactly what he had hoped to find.

His shovel blade turned up a flattened leaf of flint. The tip was broken, but enough remained to show it had been shaped by human hand, carefully sharpened, and artfully grooved. It had been, in fact, a weapon; a weapon specifically designed to kill a massive animal that had ceased to exist a hundred centuries before America was "discovered." To the man with the shovel— Jerry Dawson, a graduate assistant in the Department of Anthropology of the University of New Mexico and an "Early Man" specialist—the broken weapon was confirmation of what the flint chips had hinted. Dawson had found the trail of a mysterious Stone Age hunter who had stalked the long-horned bison in an era when the ice walls of the retreating glaciers still chilled the American West. Dawson's shovel had cut through ten thousand years of time and uncovered the hunting camp of Folsom Man.

Our continent had been cooler and wetter when the hunter untied the thong on the haft of his lance and discarded the broken point here. He was wrapped in animal skins, because the chilly rain clouds still moved across the plains from the melting glaciers to the north. The broken point may have meant that the man—and the woman he had collected—slept hungry that night. It tells us that the hunter's lance had missed his target and struck the stony ground. He could not miss often and live.

Hunger would make him too weak for the marathon runs to head off the grazing herds and find places of ambush, and too weak to avoid the six-foot horn span of the massive Taylor's Bison when they charged. When he was weak the other hunters would come for him, for the age of glaciers had made North America a veritable zoo of strange and exotic animals and he was only one of the many meat-eating predators. The age science calls "Pleistocene" produced in the American West three species of jaguar, the lion-sized saber-tooth cat, huge bears, and bone-eating dogs. Worst of all, there were the Dire Wolves, oversize killers that modern science would label, with descriptive simplicity, "The Terrible Wolf." We know that sometimes Folsom Man killed these great wolves. Sometimes, undoubtedly, they killed him.

If the broken point meant that the Ice Age bison were becoming scarce and elusive on this sloping ridge, it would also mean Folsom Man would soon be leaving—continuing the wanderings which took him up and down the empty continent from Alberta, Canada, to northern Mexico and, some clues indicate, as far east as Virginia and Georgia.

Anthropologists know of his travels from his kill sites, buried now under eons of dust and silt, scattered up and down the east slope of the Rocky Mountains. From these they know how he killed, skinned, and butchered his game, how he made his weapons, and something of his cunning tactics as a hunter. Through dating procedures based on knowledge of geological strata in the earth and on the rate of radioactive decay of a carbon element in ashes and bones, they have placed him approximately in the immense dimension of time. Beyond this there is only a scattering of evidence and some educated guessing.

We can guess that he was a large man, because the age of ice tended to exaggerate size in the animals it spawned, because Cro-Magnon Man, his brother in Europe, was a bulky individual, and because the way he found to survive on a hostile planet demanded great strength. We can also guess that he was equipped with the "stomach folds" common among aboriginal hunting tribes which gorge when they make a kill and endure hunger when they don't. We can guess, too, that he was "long headed," with a narrow skull still sometimes found in modern men.

But we can only guess, because not a fragment of his skeleton has ever been found. For some baffling reason, anthropologists who uncover the boneyards of the great animals he killed find not as much as a tooth of the mighty hunter who butchered them. And in this mystery, scientists believe they have a clue to his character.

The man who camped on this hillside probably decided for himself when his life must end—and then deliberately exposed himself to death. When he reached old age (and for him, as for the professional athlete, old age came at thirty-five or forty) he would leave his hunting band and go out to be killed and eaten by the wolves. The Masai in Kenya and some primitive Eskimo people still practice this grisly form of suicide when they can no longer contribute to the tribe. Masai bones are not found because the hyenas follow the lions and destroy the skeletons. The bone-eating dogs of the Ice Age would have followed the saber-tooth cats and the Dire Wolves.

But while no trace remains of Folsom Man himself, his hunting routes are littered with clues to his being. We know he cut a flat disk from bison bone and carved markings in its edges. We know his tools tended to be smaller and far better finished than was common among Stone Age people. We know he used fire to stampede game, and how he made his tools, and how he used them. But for every fact, there are a dozen questions. Why did he carve the disk? Why did he design a lance tip with features that seem to defy common sense? Why did he spend so much time building beauty into a weapon as expendable as a rifle bullet? Why did he make this lance point in exactly this same difficult, unchanging pattern down through a thousand years of time and fifty human generations? And, above all, why did the day come about ten thousand years ago when broken Folsom Points were no longer being dropped at campsites and left, unbroken, among the bones of bison? Why did the man who once camped on the Llano de Albuquerque vanish from the earth?

When I arrived at the site where Jerry Dawson was hunting answers to questions like these, the ridge had been pegged off into ten-foot squares, their boundaries marked by white string. Near the top of the ridge, most of these squares had been stripped of topsoil, exposing a hard, pockmarked surface. Dawson was down the slope, creating an impressive plume of dust as he shook dirt through a sifter frame.

I had heard of Dawson and the dig from Dr. Frank Hibben, a professor of anthropology at the University of New Mexico. Hibben, a famous figure for years in the hunt for Early Man and director of the Folsom Man project, told me that Dawson was thirty-nine and a crack field man. He had returned to the university for graduate studies after working as a power plant engineer on the Navajo Indian Reservation and as maintenance engineer at Martin Marietta Corporation plants in New Mexico and Colorado. Dawson had a solid background in archaeology, having worked as salvage archaeologist for the Acoma, Laguna, and Chiricahua Apache Indians. Now he was Hibben's graduate assistant and, since early spring, had been assigned to handle fieldwork on the Folsom Man dig called the "Rio Rancho Site."

As Hibben had predicted, Dawson seemed glad enough to have a visitor. "First," he said, "I'll show you some of the stuff I'm finding. Then we'll take a break and I'll give you the guided tour of the layout." He worked the remaining clods through the screen with his trowel and then carefully raked out an accumulation of buffalo grass and young tumbleweeds. The residue caught on the wire included an assortment of twigs and roots, half a dozen dried antelope droppings, a large, badly confused scorpion, and several hundred small bits of gravel. Dawson poked through this debris with a calloused finger.

"Here's one," he said. He held up a paper-thin chip of white stone, no larger than a fingernail clipping, and, to my layman's eye, in no way remarkable from five hundred other fragments of rock on the screen.

Dawson laughed. "One more piece of Folsom workshop debris. The stuff he chipped off while sharpening a lance point." He turned the chip over in his fingers. "This happens to be a pressure flake. Here," he said, indicating a tiny marred spot on the chip, "is where he applied his tool to punch it off."

He salvaged one more chip, made some cryptic-looking notes on an envelope, dropped the stones into it, and filed it with scores of others in one of those canvas handbags the airlines give away. Dawson explained that the envelopes were keyed to the individual grids into which the site was divided, "so I can sit down later, map it all out, and know where we found what."

He shook the sand out of a paper cup, handed me a drink of warm water from a ten-gallon can, and suggested we take a look around the site.

"I still don't know exactly what we have here," Dawson said, as we crossed the stripped area near the top of the ridge. "We're walking on the Folsom Floor—the surface that he lived on. I'm cleaning this off here and there to see what I find. So far, it looks like some sort of a pattern is developing, but I'm not sure what it means."

At the top of the ridge, Dawson said, the camp's lookouts must have squatted, watching the thousands of acres of rolling grassland below for bison herds. While they watched, they removed the butts of lance points, broken on their last excursion, from their lance shafts and replaced them with new points. Dawson had found the broken butts where they had been dropped, but no broken tips—which would have been found if the points had been spoiled at the spot during manufacture. In the same area he had found large splinters of flint, the sort which would be cracked off by hammering in roughing out a larger block of stone into a "blank" ready for sharpening and finishing.

Oddly absent were the little flint hide scrapers that archaeologists expect to find at Folsom campsites.

And, although the splinters indicated the hilltop had been used as a workshop, the tiny chips Folsom Man made in the meticulous finishing of his weapons were also missing.

"I've finally begun finding a few of those pressure flaking chips, like the one you saw, down the hill," Dawson said. "Maybe that means another party came along and camped down there, or maybe it means water erosion drifted the fine material, or maybe it means something else. It's just possible we may find something that will finally tell us a little about how they lived in camp. That's why I'm taking it slow and careful. I don't want to destroy any evidence."

On the way back to the wheelbarrow, I told Dawson I had some questions: How, in the immense landscape spread around us, did he happen to choose this spot to explore?

Dawson grinned. "I'd like to tell you that we worked it out by logic, and I guess we might have because in some ways this is a logical place for a hunting camp. From up here he could overlook the grazing routes. He could see them coming, and move ahead of them with his hunting blinds, and set up his ambush. But actually we found this place because we had some good luck."

Dawson said an amateur archaeologist named Wayne Stell, exploring the area in search of Indian arrowheads, noticed handworked flint in an erosion blowout, and recognized the artifacts as Folsom material. Stell reported the find to the University of New Mexico and Hibben initiated a search of the area.

"We were lucky it was Stell, someone who knows the business, because he recognized Folsom workmanship," Dawson said. "And we're lucky it came to the attention of someone who knows as much about the primitive hunters as Hibben. Otherwise, it might have been missed."

The first surveys made of the vicinity after Stell's discovery had not looked promising. But this ridgeline, with its long view of thousands of acres of grazing land and its position commanding likely routes for bison, had seemed worthy of a special investigation. Hibben had assigned Dawson, an experienced field man, to check it out.

"I guess we're also lucky we found a camping place," Dawson said. "Several kill sites have been uncovered, but just a couple of little camps—and this one is beginning to look fairly big."

Dawson fished into his shirt pocket, extracted a leaf-shaped piece of pink flint perhaps two inches long, and handed it to me. "We're lucky, too, that Folsom Man hunted with something as easy to recognize as this. Almost everything about it is different from the work of other Stone Age people—and with some rare exceptions, he always made it this way: same shape, same size, same features."

The flint had been flattened to a quarter-inch thickness by something which left parallel grooves in the face of the stone. A long groove, extending almost to the tip, had been gouged out of each face—like the blood channels on a modern bayonet. The base was slightly concave, with an ear of stone protruding from each side. And the point and edges had been given a knifelike sharpness by the chipping away of tiny flakes.

"You might say this point is the solution to a problem," Dawson said. "He needed a way to kill long-horned bison, which was faster than he was, plenty tough, and probably plenty dangerous for a man on foot. He came up with this. This point solved his problem but it left us with a tough one to work out."

The problem confronting the anthropologists was why Folsom Man always hollowed the face of his lance points by cutting out channel flakes, and why he took the added trouble of making them with ears protruding from the base. These features made the point much more difficult to manufacture. They also produced an effect which common sense indicated the hunter would try to avoid.

Because of its size (too small for a spear), and because points were often found smashed by terrific impact, anthropologists were sure the Folsom Point had been designed for a throwing lance and launched from an atlatl—a device still used by the Australian aborigines. About two feet long, with a notch at one end to fit the base of the lance and finger thongs at the other, the atlatl serves as an extension of the hunter's arm and gives him a tremendous increase in throwing leverage. Dawson said that Dick Marshall, another graduate assistant at the university, had thrown a lance point through an inch of seasoned oak at one-hundred-foot range while experimenting with one.

"It's clear enough how he slammed his lance into the bison, and why he didn't seem to bother to aim at the soft spots," Dawson said. "But what happened then is a nice little puzzle."

The ears protruding from the base of the lance point would obviously have caught inside the animal and the fluting would have made it easier to pull the lance off the point—leaving it lost inside the victim.

"There doesn't seem to be any practical reason he would want this to happen. You'd think he would want to pull the lance shaft out with the head still attached, so he could use it again without retipping it." Arrows, which developed later, with their much lighter impact and different purpose, were usually designed to hang in the wound so they might work deeper and eventually kill. But not hard-hitting lances.

"And yet he must have planned it this way. He left the Folsom Point in the animal even when he butchered it—even when he could have gotten it out by just reaching in and taking it. Why?"

I admitted I couldn't imagine why.

"We suspect that it might have been some sort of exchange system. He gave the animal—the animal which fed him—this beautifully made point in exchange for its meat. That's not the sort of theory we can prove," Dawson said, "but nothing else makes much sense."

As we walked back to the wheelbarrow, Dawson said this was only part of the puzzle of the Folsom Point. A piece of work this sophisticated and stylized must have gradually evolved, probably through a process of trial and error. Yet, with one possible basis for argument, no evolutionary points have ever been found anywhere. No forerunners, only the fine, proved design. "And that leaves us with a couple of big questions. Where did he come from? And what happened to him?"

Anthropology has been facing such questions for less than forty years. Until 1927, it was virtually a dogma of science that man was a newcomer to the Americas. He could not have evolved here, since the Western Hemisphere had no apelike higher primates. And he could not have immigrated—it seemed—because the Great Continental Ice Sheet blocked the only route from Asia across the Bering Straits. Research proved that the Aztec and Mayan ruins in Central and South America were built long after the Christian era and the great Pueblo Indian towns and cliff dwellings of the Southwest were equally new. Thus, with a few maverick exceptions, anthropologists accepted the theory that man had not invaded the New World until perhaps a thousand years before the time of Christ.

Folsom Man demolished this theory through his odd and wasteful habit of leaving his lance head in the body of his victims. A crew from the Denver Museum was salvaging skeletons of long-extinct Taylor's Bison from an arroyo near Folsom, New Mexico. Among the bones of these Ice Age animals, under nine feet of earth, they found delicate and deadly little stone points obviously made by man. There was also evidence that the bison had been skinned and butchered. The impossible was true, and the hunt was on.

Anthropologists now know that Folsom Man was neither the first nor the last of the Stone Age hunting people in America. It is certain now that when the great ice caps accumulated on the Northern Hemisphere, the shrinking ocean level exposed a land bridge across the Bering Straits. Pleistocene animals, the mastodon, mammoth, musk ox, and dozens of other breeds, grazed across from Siberia. Man followed, probably about thirty thousand years ago, surviving amid the ice and finding his way southward along the glacier-free river valleys.

In the 1930s extensive evidence was uncovered near Clovis, New Mexico, that humans using another cruder and heavier type of stone weapon had ambushed and killed at least four woolly mammoths—an animal larger than the Asian elephant. Dating at this kill site and at others found later indicated that Clovis Man was on the hunt as early as thirteen thousand years ago and perhaps as late as ten thousand. The horizon for early man in America was pushed further back in 1941, when Dr. Hibben explored a cave in the Sandia Mountains. Under the hard ochre floor of the cave he found fossil bones and thirty-eight crude one-shouldered stone points similar to weapons used by a Stone Age culture of

Central Europe. "Sandia Man" was dated twenty thousand to twenty-five thousand years ago, because it was believed the ochre cave floor had been formed in a period of torrential rains between two glacial advances. Hibben and others now feel this dating may have been too early, but obviously Sandia Man was a much older American than Folsom.

The gap between the Indian cultures and Folsom Man is also being closed from the other end. The great "field schools" pioneered by the University of New Mexico have unlocked many mysteries. The history of American man can now be traced backward through four stages of Pueblo building civilizations, to the cliff dwellers, and beyond them to the Basket Makers. These pit dwellers first mastered the rudiments of agriculture and allowed men to end their wanderings after game and begin what we call civilization.

But before this incipient civilization, which originated less than two thousand years ago, there were thousands of years when the continent was occupied only by tiny bands of nomads. Some, in a grouping science calls the "Cochise culture," augmented their diet by gathering and grinding seeds. Some lived only by the hunt. Some of these can be traced backward in time to within a thousand years of the Folsom hunters, but their weapons and stoneworking techniques were utterly different.

"So it looks like we have some possible ancestors for Folsom, and some possible descendants," Dawson said. "The trouble is, we can't make the connections. Clovis Man looks promising. For some reason he liked to hunt mammoths instead of bison, but there is at least some similarity in the shape of his points."

Dawson declined my offer to relieve him at the shovel. He explained that it took experience to feel the difference in soil textures at the level of the Folsom "floor" and he didn't want to risk missing something, or spoiling something, by having the shovel blade cut too deep or too shallow. I was assigned to the trowel instead and given an unnecessary warning about scorpions.

Dawson worked with tireless precision. Two hours, three grid squares, and fifteen wheelbarrows of dirt later we paused to tap the water can, smoke a cigarette, and assess the situation. We had found an unfinished lance point, split during the manufacture, an increasing number of flint flakes, most of them tiny, and a broken fragment of a tooth, which Dawson identified as once belonging to "some sort of grass eater." While we smoked, Dawson matched some of the larger chips against the broken tip. If he was beginning to guess right, he said, there should be a workshop area about where we had been digging, but finding the broken point didn't mean a thing unless some of the chips matched it. I wondered why not.

"Let's say you've done a lot of work on one of these things—just about finished it. Then you put your bone chisel against the base to tap out the last channel flute and when you rap the chisel with your rock hammer, the point splits. So what do you do? You say a four-letter word and throw it about fifty feet. And that's very likely what he did, if they had four-letter words that early. So the spot we found it isn't necessarily where he was making it."

I couldn't fault Dawson's reasoning, but it proved to be wrong. The third chip he matched against the point fit perfectly into the hafting channel. Since we had found this beside the point, Dawson was now confident that his Folsom hunter had squatted to work on his weapon where we had been digging. It seemed highly improbable that the Folsom stonesmith would have recovered the channel flake from the ground to throw it after the point, or that they would have landed in the same spot if he had.

Dawson continued turning the broken point in his fingers, as if he expected this piece of rock to reveal some secret. "Well," he said finally, "take a look at this." On one side of the lance point—the face from which the hafting flute had not been removed—he put his fingernail against an almost hairline abrasion on the stone surface. It extended from the butt up the surface of the point, approximately parallel to its cutting edge.

"That's the channel guide," Dawson explained. "He cut that to control the way the channel flake split out." Dawson seemed well pleased with this discovery, and I confessed I couldn't imagine why.

"Sort of thing that might be helpful," Dawson said. "Maybe not, but it might turn out that when we take a close look at the stuff we're finding, we'll discover that the points made right here have this sort of guide, and points made somewhere else are cut in a different fashion. It's one more thing that might give us some sort of clue."

I recalled a copy of a Folsom Point, shown me by Dr. Hibben, which a graduate student had attempted to chip out of glass. Although glass is much easier to work with than flint and the student had spent tedious hours on the job, the finished product looked crude and misshapen beside the original—like an untalented amateur's attempt to copy a work of art.

"It's obvious that he did a lot more work on these points than he needed just to kill an animal," Dawson agreed. "And we notice he was also unusually choosy about the sort of material he used. Hunting people usually didn't care how it looked if it would flake off and form a sharp edge. But Folsom seemed to hunt good colors and fine grain."

He pointed westward, where a line of dunes as high as a four-story building blocked the horizon some three miles away.

"Perfect example right over there," Dawson said. "Those dunes have blown up over the breaks which drop down into the Rio Puerco valley. Behind them there are big deposits of petrified wood in plain view. Other Stone Age people loved the stuff but it wasn't good enough for Folsom. He left it alone and hauled his stone in here from God knows how far away."

Dawson said that in light of the broken point and the large number of chips uncovered in the past two hours, he was beginning to change his theories about the layout of the site. "But if we don't begin finding some hide scrapers down the slope here my theories won't be worth much."

Thirty minutes later, he had his first scraper—and within an hour two more. The grid Dawson had chosen for resumed operations was three squares—or thirty feet—south of the point where the thick scattering of chips had indicated a workshop area. Grass and topsoil were thicker here, slowing the clearing work and keeping me busy breaking up root-held clods with the trowel. But Dawson spotted the scraper when it hit the wire. He extracted it from the dirt, wiped it on his shirt sleeve, and then took it to the water can for a careful rinsing. It was a heavy flake of quartzite, about twice the size of a silver dollar, and Dawson identified it immediately as a "snub-nosed end scraper."

I mentioned that it looked to me like just another piece of flint.

"He held it like this," said Dawson, with the stone gripped between a horny thumb and the inside of his first finger, "and scraped with this side. Under a glass you can easily see the wear on the flint from the scraping. They lose their fine edge fast."

The same shovel of dirt also contained a stone knife—an even larger flake of quartzite with its cutting edge sharpened by pressure flaking. And the next scrapers turned up only a few feet away—across the string in the adjoining grid. They were another, slightly smaller, end scraper and a longer, bulky model which Dawson called a "side scraper." By then, I was ready to retire for the day from active archaeology, and my host had become confident enough in his new theory to tell me about it.

He had been puzzled, he said, by the lack of fine workshop material and scrapers at the top of the ridge—where he had found point bases and larger rough-work chips—since cleaning hides and making new points would be necessary operations at a hunting camp. Adding to the puzzle were the large quantities of workshop chips far down the slope.

"Maybe that's a second campsite," Dawson said. "Or maybe he sat up here and did his heavy hammering where the flying splinters wouldn't hit a kid and moved down to his living area to do the finishing work. If that was true, I figured we should find wornout hide scrapers down there, too, because that should be where the women cleaned the hides."

I noted that it had worked out just right to fit the second theory, and asked Dawson why he didn't look happier about it.

"In the first place," Dawson said, "we won't know we're right until we can get a geological check on the erosion. Maybe those chips washed down there. And then we have to take a hard look at these chips to see how the flint matches the big stuff on the ridge. And then, if we didn't have erosion and the chips tell us we had a lot of long-term living here, we've got ourselves another problem."

Dawson stared toward the Rio Grande, a bright ribbon of green far to the east and a thousand feet below.

"What did he do for water?" he asked. "It's at least ten miles down there and ten miles back, and that adds up to a long way to send your women after something to drink. If this camp was as big as it's beginning to look, we're going to have to find a water supply somewhere around here."

A month later, at midsummer, the water supply puzzle remained unsolved. Dawson's grid of pegs and strings had expanded now and his pile of dump earth had become a hill in its own right. I found him, almost always, working along, methodically shoveling his way through the grids from dawn until early afternoon, and then spending the hotter hours walking, eyes down, across the countryside in search of traces of ancient springs or more Folsom material.

But while Dawson was alone on his hillside, he was not alone in the field. Summer is hunting season for anthropologists.

In the mountains above Taos, a University of New Mexico field school of more than sixty students, professors, and visiting scientists was excavating a pithouse settlement of Basket Makers. In Wyoming, a task force from Harvard and the National Geographic Society was digging in Hell's Gap and finding evidence that a Stone Age hunter had stalked his game there. In eastern Canada, the Canadian National Museum was uncovering the kill sites of Clovis Man, and in southern Arizona, a University of Arizona team was exploring the Snaketown site and adding new information about the ancient Hohokam farming culture.

After a parting strategy conference on the Rio Rancho dig, Hibben had left to hunt traces of early man in East Africa. Froelich Rainey and Douglas Anderson, two University of Pennsylvania professors, were digging through nine feet of silted earth at a caribou ford on Alaska's Kobuk River and uncovering the northernmost hunting camp ever found. And above the Arctic Circle, along the Utakak River at North America's land's end, Robert Humphrey, Jr., of the University of New Mexico, was finding Stone Age tools and workshop debris which may help link early man in America to ancient Eurasian people.

The bits and pieces of information collected at these and a dozen other digs would be put together in the scholarly journals during the winter months. And as summer ended, a message came from Dawson that hinted he might have something important to add.

The afternoon before the message came, a thunderstorm had moved out of the west across the Llano de Albuquerque. High winds swept the site where Folsom Man had camped, a site now stripped of the topsoil which had protected it for thousands of years. When the storm had passed, one of this ancient hunter's secrets had been laid bare. Dawson's message said nothing of this—only that he had something to show me.

When I arrived, a pickup truck was parked at the site. Dawson and a slender young man wearing boots, horned-rimmed glasses, a cigar, and a blue shirt were leaning on its hood comparing a map with an aerial photograph.

Dawson introduced the blue-shirted man as Wayne Lambert,

a University of New Mexico geologist, and told me that Lambert's tests had indicated erosion had not effected the distribution of chips at the site. He left Lambert to ponder the map, and led me toward the crest. Just above the point where we had been digging on my first visit he stopped and indicated the ground.

"What do you think caused that?" he asked.

The earth in front of us was faintly discolored. It was also, I noticed, slightly depressed, with both the depression and the darker shade of dirt forming an oval shape, perhaps eight feet in length. If the father of all elephants had sat down heavily on the spot he might have made such a compaction. The only reasonable explanation I could think of for both the depression and the changed color of earth was that the site had been the earthen floor of a tent, occupied by sloppy eaters. "That's the only way I can explain it," Dawson said. "And if we're right, we're looking at the first sign ever found that Folsom Man lived in shelters."

As might be expected, Dawson looked pleased. "There's another one right over here."

The second discolored spot was a twin of the first in both size and axis of the oval, indicating that if they had been some sort of skin shelter, they had faced the same direction.

"They didn't show up until that high wind," Dawson said. "It cut away the sand and dust, and the change in color showed up, and then I noticed the impaction." Dawson said he would make a careful check of the artifacts and workshop debris which came out of these grids to determine if it would give any hint of the directions the shelters, if such they were, had faced.

"And there's a faint possibility we can find some evidence of post holes—some sign of displacement of the soil. Otherwise, we're going to have a hell of a time coming up with anything but inferential evidence. We'll just be able to describe what we found, where we found it, report on probable ground cover conditions when it was formed, and say what we think it is so people working other sites will know what to be looking for."

It seemed utterly impossible that Dawson could even guess about ground cover on the slope when the depressions were made and I said so. Dawson laughed.

"Actually, it's fairly simple. You think maybe wind erosion caused them, as it caused the little blowout holes around here. But wind erosion happens in extreme drought, when the grass cover is dead and gone. And when the grass is gone and it rains, the pebbles on this hillside wash downhill and collect in the blowout pits. So you check to see if pebbles also washed into these depressions."

"No pebbles," I said, knowing when I'm a loser.

"Clay," Dawson said. "The sort of stuff rainwater dissolves out when the grass is holding the topsoil. So we can infer that the oval areas were surrounded by grass when they were formed, and for a long time afterward."

Dawson said the apparent presence of shelters, probably made by stretching bison skins over poles, supported a growing collection of evidence that the ridge had been a long-term camping site. He said that three different types of flint he had been finding in three different patterns indicated that the ridge site had been used as an encampment on at least three occasions.

"And two more camping sites—maybe three—have turned up over there," Dawson said, pointing to the flat expanse of grass several hundred yards to the west. "The one I've had time to check was fairly extensive, and it's looking like this place drew Folsom hunting parties like politicians flocking to a barbecue."

Dawson said he had pretty well exhausted the possibility of old springs in the area and that Lambert had brought a topographical map and aerial photograph to check on the possibility that—in wetter times—surface water might have collected somewhere in the area.

When we returned to the pickup truck, Lambert was scrutinizing the aerial photograph through a magnifying glass. He explained he was trying to locate the dig site on the photo so he could spot it exactly on the map. Dawson peered over his shoulder.

"That's probably a photograph of Australia," Dawson said. "Trouble with having to work with geologists is they're careless about small details."

Lambert satisfied himself he had our hillside spotted, marked the point on the topographical map, and persuaded Dawson the location was correct. "You can teach an anthropologist how to dig a hole," Lambert grumbled, "but nobody's been able to teach 'em to read maps." He and Dawson bent over the chart, tracing the lines which marked the water drainage and the contour of the rolling landscape. Within thirty minutes, their interest had centered on an area about a quarter-mile west of where we were standing. Here, the topographical lines indicated a flat area surrounded by higher terrain but now drained in rainy weather by an arroyo.

"Might have been a playa," Dawson said.

"Looks like it might have been," Lambert agreed, "but the outlet is cut down enough now to keep it drained."

A mile south on the map, the two found another telltale pattern of lines indicating a second natural depression where water might have formed a shallow lake in wetter times.

Lambert discarded his dwindling cigar and picked up a long-handled boring auger. He said he would walk down to the outlet of the nearest depression and take soil samples to determine if it had once been a playa filled with water. He paused to cover the cigar butt neatly with earth.

"An anthropologist will dig that up some day and we'll be reading a learned article about how Stone Age Man was addicted to nicotine," he said.

"With a footnote reporting he rolled his own cigars out of old tennis shoes," Dawson added.

Lambert left, grinning, and Dawson and I walked across the hillside to overlook the other end of the grassy depression which might have been—thousands of years ago—a shallow marshy lake. En route we passed the second campsite Dawson had found. His surveying stakes and a gridwork of twine were in place, but only a dozen of the squares had been excavated.

"All this is beginning to make sense now," Dawson said slowly, looking out across the depression to the west. Water, he said, would have drawn the bison herds here as they moved, with the seasons, north and south along the Rio Grande Valley. From his campsite on the reverse slope of the ridge, the Folsom hunter looked down over Arroyo de las Cabalacillas (Arroyo of the Little Gourds) and on another smaller drainage course up which bison almost certainly would have moved. Grazing animals tend to follow fairly regular routes—routes offering a minimum of obstacles.

If this depression did prove to be the site of an ancient playa, Dawson went on, he'd probably be able to find additional camp-sites in the area surrounding it. The shoreline would have to be established and surveyed for possible bone deposits—since bones buried in mud are often preserved. And then there was the possi-bility of other plays with more camps. These would be unusually important, Dawson said, because the original well-preserved site provided an excellent reference against which they could be checked.

"That first site is going to tell us a lot when I get time to ana-lyze what we're finding. I think we're going to have some hint of whether he lived in a small family unit, how many families in a camp, and know quite a bit more about how he hunted, and that will give us some clues to how he thought." Dawson said the site had already produced at least five hundred stone points and tools of all types and several thousand bits and pieces of workshop de-bris. At the richest Folsom find in history, the famous Linden-meier kill site in northern Colorado, a joint task force from the Smithsonian Institution and the Denver Museum of Natural His-tory collected only a few more tools and chipping in a four-year operation.

I asked Dawson what he meant by checking one site against another.

"Remember that broken point we found—the one with one channel flute split out and the guide cut for the second one? Well," Dawson said, "at this second site, the point butts showed a different sort of guide. Instead of cutting it parallel with the sides of the point, these boys slanted it diagonally. And they liked to use a different sort of flint. We may be able to get enough to infer they were from a different group or the same group at a different time. Or, if we're lucky enough, we might find some traces of evolution in the point design."

The possibility of finding a widespread complex of Folsom hunting camps had jolted Dawson out of his habitual caution. He speculated on the chance of finally locating some clue to link Folsom with the earlier hunters—or some hint of why and how their culture vanished from the earth.

"That business of shelters is interesting," Dawson said. "If that's what they were, they had to be covered with bison hides. And I don't think they would pack something that heavy around with them. They would cache the hides and use them again when they made the swing back through the territory the next year."

Dawson anticipated my question. "Who would steal them? He had the world pretty much to himself. If they left the shelter hides at camp, that might mean they had a semipermanent network of camping sites up and down the river. That'll be something to check out."

Under the blistering early September sun, this prospect of an endless series of additional Folsom sites seemed to me remarkably cheerless—promising Dawson an infinite supply of dirt to be shoveled and dust to eat. Yet he spoke of it with obvious enthusiasm.

In the American university system, where the supply of brainy young men working for the Doctor of Philosophy degree drastically exceeds demands for their services, graduate assistants like Dawson lead notoriously lean and ragged lives. I asked Dawson about this. Why leave an easier, well-paid job for the ordeal of research? What had kept him hunting ghosts on this hillside through the hot summer? And how could he look happily forward to more of the same?

"The answer is even longer than your question," Dawson said. "Take a look at this Folsom Man. Everything he did was important—the way he made his point, the way he balanced his lance, the way he set up his ambush. If he didn't do it right, his family starved, or maybe a bison gored him. I never enjoyed doing a job which, if I stopped to think of it, didn't matter if it got done or not."

Dawson said he felt that what anthropologists were doing was important. While modern man knows a great deal about many things, he knows very little about himself and his long history on the planet.

"This Folsom Man had to be a pretty select specimen, both physically and mentally. To hunt the animals he did on foot he had to be fast, and agile, and plenty smart. The ones who weren't, wouldn't survive, and so he had selective breeding working for him for generations. And yet we know that one day Folsom Man wasn't around any more. Something went wrong. We don't know what and I think we should know. I think it's important to know everything we can about man, and most of his million or so years on earth he's been a hunter, like Folsom."

Dawson stopped, apparently embarrassed at catching himself in the act of philosophizing. "I must also admit," he said with a grin, "that I don't like to sit on my rear in an office when I can be outdoors."

It was the first and only time I had managed to prod Dawson into talking about himself, and Lambert gave him an excuse to change the subject by walking up. The outlet of the basin had been higher once, he reported, high enough to hold back a substantial but shallow lake. He had found some sign of lakebed sedimentation, and the other basin to the south also seemed promising.

Dawson headed back for his shovel, looking immensely pleased.

How Quemado Got Quemado

"This was just a little dinky place then," says the man waiting at the service station in Quemado, "and it didn't even have a name. Then one morning Geronimo and his Apaches came riding through and after that they took to calling it Quemado."

"There's another more official version that says the creek where this Catron County village is located was named Rito Quemado because a brush fire had blackened both its banks. But the cowboy's explanation of why a village comes to be named "Burned" has more laconic poetry.

And then, north over the Zuni Mountains and beyond Grants, there is Ambrosia Lake, which has given its name to the surrounding uranium mining district—America's largest. Irony here, one thinks. The source of fuel for nuclear desolation named Ambrosia, the perfume and nectar of the gods. But Matt Pearce tells us in *New Mexico Place Names* that the word should be

Ambrosio, which was the name of the settler whose body was found floating in its waters, thereby causing it to be identified as "la laguna del Ambrosio Difunto."

The dictionary does odd things to a bilingual landscape. Because the Anglo-American postmaster could not pronounce the Spanish *i* the settlement of *Anil* became *Anal* in the U.S. Postal Guide, on postmarks, and finally on the map of Guadalupe County. The post office is closed now (to the relief, one suspects, of those charged with preventing the movement of obscene words by the U.S. mails), but the misspelling lives on, an adjective become a name which only towns in Texas deserve.

6

Las Trampas

✫

At the village of Santo Tomás del Rio de las Trampas, thirty-five miles by air north and east of the New Mexico State Capitol buildings at Santa Fe, death is personified as a hooded skeleton. She rides a cart with high wooden wheels and is known with familiarity, and even affection, as Doña Sebastiana. Except during Holy Week, Doña Sebastiana remains parked in a small, iron-roofed structure adjoining the northeast corner of the Church of San José de Gracia. The building is the *morada* of the village Penitente Brotherhood. For many generations Doña Sebastiana and her cart have been taken from this lodging on Good Friday and pulled by two of the Brothers of the Light in procession around the village plaza. She holds in her bony hands a drawn bow and, according to legend, will release her arrow if the cart passes an unrepentant sinner.

Doña Sebastiana is a product of the Middle Ages, a mixture of the "little sister Death" of Saint Francis of Assisi and the preoccupation of Medieval Europe with penitence and dissolution. She is an anachronism in the twentieth century and remains very much at home among the Trampaseños only because this little settlement in the Sangre de Cristo Mountains of New Mexico is still closer to the Age of Faith than to the Age of Reason.

Until relatively recent times this was true of all of the Spanish-Colonial settlements in the mountains named for the Blood of Christ. They were the last and most distant outposts flung out by a dying Spanish empire. And while their physical link with the world was the risky two-thousand-mile road to Mexico City, their more vital link was with the Spain of Cervantes, Lope de Vega, and Calderón, of mystics, saints, and conquistadores, a Spain that had ceased to exist before they were founded.

For the settlements in the richer low valleys, the Middle Ages ended abruptly after the United States occupied New Mexico in 1847. The change was slower for the poorer high villages, coming only when they were connected to the present with well-traveled roads. These brought with them bars, gasoline pumps, motels, tourist shops, and some small relief from traditional poverty. At Las Trampas, neither the past nor the poverty has yet been affected by asphalt pavement. The only road which reaches it is of dirt.

The village in the high valley of the Rio de las Trampas has always been an out-of-the-way place. It was bypassed as thoroughly by the eighteenth and nineteenth centuries as it is by the twentieth. When it was established in 1751 it was on El Camino Alto, the "high road" between the Spanish capital at Santa Fe and the northernmost outpost of colonial bureaucracy at Alcaldía de Taos. This road was a poor detour linking the mission church at the big, and often troublesome, Picuris Indian Pueblo and a scattering of impoverished high-country settlements. It was rough and slow and often closed by winter snows. It was also dangerous. Comanche raiding parties, crossing the mountain passes from the buffalo plains of eastern New Mexico to collect cattle, scalps, and slaves from the Spanish and their Pueblo Indian allies, could and did ambush this route with little risk of pursuit.

The concern for Indians along the Camino Alto was a principal reason Las Trampas was settled. Only a few years earlier a Comanche war party had moved through Palo Flechado Pass to the north, besieged and captured a fortified rancho, killed its thirteen male defenders, and carried away more than sixty women and children. Their raids at Picuris, just nine miles north of Las Trampas, had become so frequent and daring that the settlers tore down their church and rebuilt it at a more defensible location. A village at Las Trampas would, at least in theory, impede one route for marauders crossing the Sangre de Cristo range to loot the Santa Cruz Valley below. Most of this valley was owned by Captain Sebastián Martín Serrano, a noted swordsman, who had been granted his vast holdings in 1712 by King Philip V as a reward for his exploits as an Indian fighter. By mid-century, the captain was old and ready to leave the fighting to others. He granted land in the high Las Trampas, Ojo Sarco, and de los Alamos valleys for a new settlement, and arrangements were made by Governor Vélez Cachupín for an additional royal grant of 46,000 acres to give the community woodcutting and grazing land.

In the context of the times the grant must not have seemed particularly attractive. In the 1750 census the population of the vast province of Nuevo Mexico had been tallied at some forty-two hundred *gentes de razon,* a "reasonable people" category in which the Spanish included all those with any blood links to the Old World, including Negroes and mestizo Spanish-Indians. There were also some twelve thousand more-or-less tame Pueblo Indians. The shortage, thus, was not of land but of people to hold it against the sort of Indians who would not stay still for a Spanish census. In view of the precarious location of the Rio de las Trampas grant, residents of 1750 Santa Fe must have detected an irony in its title. *Trampa,* in Spanish, means "trap."

The man who proved willing to settle in the valley of the traps was Juan de Arguello, of whom we know only a little. He was seventy-four years old when he undertook this difficult venture in frontier colonization. But he still had thirty-eight years to live—time enough before he died in 1789 to build his village to its peak population of more than sixty families and to complete its landmark and its glory, the Church of San José de Gracia. We also know Arguello was born at Zacatecas, the old colonial city in the Valley of Mexico that provided New Mexico with many of its seventeenth-century soldiers and settlers. By 1715, he was at Santa Fe, being married to Juana Gregoria Brito. We know this union produced several daughters, because some of the eleven men he recruited to settle Las Trampas with him were his sons-in-law and his grandchildren were with those first in the community. We also know that others he recruited were the children and grandchildren of Sebastian Rodríguez, and this tells us that among the founding families of his village were some of Negro lineage. Rodríguez was the African drummer boy of Don Diego de Vargas Zapata Ponce de León, the famous captain-general who was driven from the province in the bloody rising of the Pueblos in 1680 and who reconquered the territory for Spain in 1693.

We know, too, that Arguello is buried in the village he founded and that the death record says this of him:

"Juan de Arguello, at the age of 112 years. Founder of the church and the village. He died in full possession of his faculties."

One of those faculties must surely have been dogged persistence. His Church of San José de Gracia is a "lay chapel," built without help from clergy or state. It took Arguello and his Trampaseños some twenty years to finish the job.

The Church of San José de Gracia looks today exactly as it did in 1780 and architectural antiquarians rate it as one of the most perfect surviving examples of Spanish-Colonial mission structures. If one needs a reason for taking the slow high road and visiting the old village, the church is reason enough.

The church was started in 1760, a year in which young George Washington, newly wed, was raising horses in the British colony of Virginia, and the year in which Bishop Pedro Tamarón of the See of Durango made the long trip north to inspect the missions on the Spanish frontier. The bishop passed through Las Trampas en route to the church at Picuris Pueblo. He reported that the villagers "approached us and begged us to be pleased to concede our license so that they might build there a chapel and church with the title and advocation of Lord Saint Joseph of Grace." Bishop Tamarón noted that the Trampaseños had a nine-mile walk "over enemy infested roads" to reach the Picuris church. He granted the villagers their license and with it the duty of maintaining "the aforesaid chapel with all possible seemliness and cleanliness."

Sixteen years later, in 1776, Arguello remained spry enough to make the long walk over the mountain ridges to Picuris. He came to ask a visiting Franciscan for alms for the church. The visitor was the famous Fray Francisco Domínguez, sent from Mexico City to inspect the Spanish borderlands. In his report, discovered among bundles of material in the Mexican National Library in 1928 and published by the University of New Mexico Press in 1956 as *The Missions of New Mexico, 1776*, Fray Domínguez provided an early view of villagers and their church.

"This chapel has been built by alms from the whole kingdom, for the citizens of this place have begged throughout it. The chief promoter in all this has been one Juan Arguello who is more than 80 years old and this man asked me for alms for the said chapel during my visitation of Picuris. And since I have nothing, I gave him that, with many thanks for his devotion." The "alms from the whole kingdom" which Fray Domínguez mentions amounted to a grand total of nine *pesos,* six *reales.*

Although the visiting priest underestimated Arguello's age (he was actually ninety-eight or ninety-nine at the time), the description he provided of the church and its setting remains, after almost two hundred years, exactly accurate. A few of the furnishings have been changed, the crossbar which then secured the front doors has been replaced with a nineteenth-century cast-iron lock, and the choir loft, then "still in the process of being made," has been completed. But there are still twenty-five beams supporting the roof of the nave, just as Domínguez counted, and nineteen above the transept, and nine above the sanctuary. The bell he described as "middle sized" still hangs in its place to the left of the entrance, singing in a deep, rich voice when tapped with the knuckles. The pulpit which to Domínguez looked "new, and badly made" still stands at the Gospel side of the sanctuary. No longer new, it has become a museum curator's dream. A small octagon with carved wooden sides, it is mounted on a pedestal hewn in corkscrew fashion from the trunk of a ponderosa pine. A rickety plank ladder provides access.

The Franciscan's old report also still serves remarkably well as a thumbnail depiction of Las Trampas valley and its inhabitants.

"This little settlement is in a cañada of the Sierra Madre," Domínguez reported. "It runs from southeast to northwest, with a small river with a very rapid current of good crystalline water in the middle. It is not half a league long, but since it is rather wide, it has fairly good farmlands on both banks of the river. Watered by this river, they yield quite reasonable crops with the exception of chile (peppers) and frijol (beans).

"These settlers do not live in ranchos but in a plaza like a neighborhood house. For the most part they are a ragged lot, but there are three or four who have enough to get along after a fashion. They are as festive as they are poor, and very merry. Accordingly, most of them are low class, and there are very few of good, or even moderately good, blood. Almost all are their own masters and servants, and in general they speak the Spanish I have described in other cases. The following includes them all: 63 families with 279 persons."

Today the count includes only thirty-four families and the farmland has given up almost two centuries of fertility. But the

Rio de las Trampas remains clear and icy, draining the melting snow from the alpine meadows of the Pecos Wilderness Area just to the east and demonstrating how little water is required in this arid climate to warrant the title "river." The valley still produces few beans, and poor chili—a minor mystery since the chiles of Chimayo, only a few ridges away, are a byword of gourmets. And the Trampaseños still speak the Spanish Domínguez found sadly typical of the frontier, the Spanish of Cervantes's Sancho Panza. It had a strange, old-fashioned sound to the priest accustomed to the more polished Gongoristic Spanish of Mexico City, and it has an archaic sound today.

The route to Las Trampas also remains unchanged, following the course dictated, now as then, by mountain terrain. The name has changed. El Camino Alto has become State Road 76. And now the trip from Santa Fe can be made in little more than an hour if the route's endless temptations to stop and look are properly resisted.

One reaches the village by driving northward from Santa Fe twenty-two miles on four-lane U.S. Highway 64-84-285. At Espanola he turns eastward up the Santa Cruz Valley toward the mountains. There are twenty-two more miles to travel and the first fourteen are paved.

Almost immediately after turning onto State Road 76, the visitor is in the scattered village of Santa Cruz, one of the oldest European settlements in what is now the United States. Old Santa Cruz, on the south bank of the little Santa Cruz River, was founded in 1598 by colonists accompanying the original army of exploration led by Oñate. La Villa Nueva de Santa Cruz, the "new town," is on the north bank of the stream. Indians of the

San Cristóbal and San Lázaro Pueblos had captured the original village in the 1680 uprising and new colonists who arrived in 1695 chose the new location. The church they built in 1733 is one of the largest such structures in New Mexico, a massive cruciform building dominating the village plaza and housing a treasury of Spanish-Colonial religious art. To Arguello and his settlers, passing through in 1751, Santa Cruz represented the last substantial outpost of safety and civilization.

Above Santa Cruz, State Road 76 winds along the north bank of the river past eight miles of adobe farmhouses and fruit orchards to Chimayo—a village of apples, lilacs, weavers, and woodcarvers. When Arguello passed, San Buenaventura de Chimayó was an insignificant place, even by frontier standards. It had been, until very recently, a point marking the extreme eastern frontier of the province, a point beyond which banished criminals were forbidden to return. Its church, the small but classic Santuario de Chimayó, was not constructed until Don Bernardo Abeyta built it as a family project in 1813.

From Chimayo, the road climbs steadily, following the crest of a narrow ridge which separates two small valleys. It skirts past Cordova, a cluster of adobe buildings far below and to the right. Cordova was an "unofficial" village, settled without bureaucratic approval at the site of a burned Indian pueblo, and only a few ranchos were there when Arguello passed. Today it is a center for wood carving and in many of its homes one can find the figures of saints and animals fashioned in the soft, stylized lines of the folk tradition from yellow pine.

Truchas lies three miles east and 1,880 feet up, and the highway, still following its narrow ridge, offers a spectacular view of mountains and empty, broken land. Truchas, which means "trout," is the highest of the old villages. It is crowded along the edge of a plateau 7,622 feet above sea level and more than a half-mile above the Rio Grande Valley to the west. Its roofs are sharply peaked against the high-country snow and behind these roofs the three Truchas peaks loom against the sky. North peak, tallest of the trio, rises to 13,102 feet. Only Mount Wheeler, 13,151 feet at its peak in the mountains behind Taos, is taller in New Mexico.

Truchas is the sister village of Las Trampas, founded only three years later and for the same motive—to hold the high passes against the Indians. Governor Vélez made this communal grant to the Romero and Espinosa families. He specifically ordered that the settlement be collected around two adjoining plazas for the common defense against the Comanches. But when the villagers petitioned for twelve muskets and a supply of gunpowder to arm themselves, their plea was pigeonholed. It remains in the archives with the word "denied" written in Spanish across its face.

In view of the chronic problems with the nomadic Indians, this policy of keeping firearms out of the hands of civilians seems strange at best. But it was adhered to both by the Spanish-Colonial administrations and the Mexican authorities who followed them. Undoubtedly the principal reason was the shortage of weapons, which frequently forced even the military to fight with bows and lances. But in view of the so-called Chimayó Revolt of 1837, in which Santa Cruz Valley settlers defeated the official militia and the governor's head was returned to Santa Fe on a pike, there may have been other motives as well.

The situation led to an odd reversal of what one has come to expect of frontier America. The Indians sold guns to the settlers. Fray Domínguez noted this in his report, indicating neither surprise nor disapproval. The Comanches would obtain muskets, pistols, powder, and lead from Eastern tribes, who had been armed by the French. They would make periodic visits to Taos to barter these weapons and buffalo hides to the Spanish and Pueblo Indians for grain, worked leather, knives, and other products—and to collect ransom for the Spanish and Pueblo women and children captured on their most recent raids. Fray Domínguez noted that one Comanche swapped a pistol for a leather bridle. Thus the citizens of Las Trampas eventually obtained five muskets from the Comanches they intended to shoot. When one stands in the village with wooded hills crowding in to within bowshot on two sides, it is easy to appreciate how important those firearms must have been. Las Trampas lies in a pocket which must have been the despair of those responsible for its defense.

To reach this little valley, State Road 76 drops more than a thousand feet in eight crooked miles from Truchas. It dips through the minuscule village of Ojo Sarco, built on what was once land of the Trampaseños, climbs the great Cañada del Ojo Sarco ridge, and Santo Tomás del Rio de las Trampas lies suddenly below, visible through the pines only moments before you reach it.

It is worth a moment's pause, before dropping into the village, to examine the patchwork of land around the community. This pattern tells why, if your trip is made in the summer, you are unlikely to see more than one or two men, why the village is without economic hope, and why the church—which for two centuries has given Las Trampas its modest grandeur and the villagers their source of pride—is not likely to survive another century. This tiny valley, plus a small and scattered allocation of grazing rights in the adjoining national forest, is all that remains of the village holdings, all that remains of a land grant of more than seventy-five square miles. The communal ownership system, efficient for production and defense, proved remarkably inefficient in coping with property taxes imported after the American occupation in 1847. A church could be built with crops, and guns bought with bridles, but paying taxes required money and the villagers had none.

From the point where State Road 76 enters Las Trampas one can see that the 210 acres of the valley—about enough for a single midwestern family farm—are divided into a hodgepodge of patches and plots. There are, in fact, sixty-six individual plots owned by the thirty-four Las Trampas families. A few are as large as eight or ten acres. Some are smaller than building lots in cheap suburban housing developments. Several are 400 or 500 yards long and only a few paces wide—allowing barely room to turn a plow horse. Time, death, and the division of family property has hopelessly gerrymandered the little left to Las Trampas.

The village has, of course, always been poor and it undertook its ambitious church-building project in the face of this poverty. Fray Domínguez reported in 1776 that Father Andrés Claremonte, the missionary at Picuris Pueblo, had authorized Arguello to collect the "first fruits" of the settlement for one year. He was to use this tithe, which then was the first one-sixth of most crops, to buy "the sacred necessities for the chapel." This tithe in crops and livestock, collected from the sixty-three families then living in the village, netted Arguello's church fund a total of sixteen pesos, one real. It is difficult to translate the value of a peso on the eighteenth-century Spanish frontier to today's dollars. We know, however, that the two simple bronze candleholders bought for the altar cost one peso each.

But while eighteenth-century Las Trampas was poor, the poverty then was above the subsistence level. The villagers were, as Fray Domínguez reported, "their own masters." Today, few are their own masters in the economic sense. The village is almost empty of men in the summer because the men are away working for others, in the beet fields of Colorado, on forest fire teams, and at jobs in the Española Valley. Las Trampas can no longer support its sons.

The situation at Las Trampas, typical as it is of all the villages of New Mexico's mountain north, is of interest to antiquarians as well as to humanitarians. When the Trampaseños are forced at last from the valley that cannot sustain them the Church of San José de Gracia will quickly fall into ruins.

State Road 76 passes within a few yards of the old church. At the bottom of the ridge it crosses a culvert through which the valley's south irrigation acequia runs and then splits the hayfield of Jose T. Lopez to reach the Rio de las Trampas bridge. In early summer, when the snowpack is still melting on Trampas Peak to the east, a lively mountain brook runs under this bridge. Later there is only a trickle of water for the village fields. Immediately over this bridge, the road bends between the homes of Enrique Lopez, Luis E. Vigil, and Mrs. Francisco Leyba to enter the plaza.

Originally, this rectangle was walled solidly with the abutting homes of the villagers. Now it is formed by an irregular array of residences on three sides and the front wall of the churchyard on the north. There is little flat ground in the narrow valley and the plaza is no exception. It slopes sharply away from the chapel and the churchyard wall serves as a retaining structure. Filled with earth, it provides a level surface around the front of the building.

Like all such village plazas, this one is of bare earth and innocent of grass, pavement, or any attempt at landscaping. The houses which hedge it are of adobe plastered with mud. All share the appearance of unguessable age characteristic of earthen structures, and most show some signs of disrepair, although several are neatly painted and plastered. Some are standing empty, a grim portent for a high-country village.

When opened, the doorway of the churchyard wall frames for the eye the front elevation of the church. Seen from this perspective, the entrance of San José de Gracia seems to be flanked by two blunt towers, towers which are largely formed by the ends of the massive side walls of the chapel. The front wall is recessed some three feet between them. It is plastered and painted white, contrasting starkly with the earthen color of the remainder of the building.

The church is virtually devoid of exterior decoration and from any angle its unbroken lines and gently sloping walls give the impression of massiveness. Long wooden *canales* jut from its flat roof to drain rainwater well away from its vulnerable adobe masonry and the plastered front is protected from above by a heavy beam surmounted by an earthen parapet.

Below this beam, the side walls are connected at the one-story level by the wooden front balcony of the choir. A wide door provides access from the inside choir loft to this balcony. Just below it are the double front doors of the church and, to the left of them, the church bell hangs from a heavy rope.

The bell is called Refugio and once had a companion named Gracia. Until Gracia was cut from its rope and stolen, about 1909, the Las Trampas bell ringer would use the low-voiced bell of refuge to announce solemn events and the soprano bell of grace for happier occasions. The death of children too young for sin would be announced, for example, by the tolling of Gracia in celebration of soul attaining heaven without enduring the trials of earth.

Except on days when services are held, the front doors are usually locked and seeing the inside of the church involves finding the key. This is passed around the village from month to month, being left in custody of the family currently responsible for sweeping, cleaning, and patching the building. Some asking around is required, but when one finds the key he will also find a guide, for Trampaseños are proud of their church.

Once through the double doors, it takes a moment for the eyes to adjust from the brilliant high-altitude sunlight of the churchyard to the dim interior of the nave. The first impression given by the Church of San José de Gracia is one of cool, dark stillness. The silence is almost cavelike, for earth is an excellent soundproofing agent, the walls are four feet thick, and even the roof overhead is insulated with a heavy layer of adobe clay. The sounds of the village—the bark of a dog and a rooster crowing—seep faintly through the high windows. And with this silence, there is the dim aroma of old incense and burned wax to tease the memory.

The nave of the church is lit only by two windows, cut above head level through the thick adobe of the east wall. The sanctuary seems at first to glow with its own light, but it too has its windows, cut even higher in the east and west ends of the clerestory. The only provision for artificial lighting in the nave is by two crude chandeliers, each made of two planks joined in the form of a cross. The planks are lined at the top with wax candles, which are lit by lowering the chandeliers from pulleys hung from ceiling beams.

The floor of the church is rough and uneven, formed of foot-wide planks, laid in sections three planks wide and some seven feet long, and worn by many generations of feet. The board ceiling is supported by twenty-five closely spaced vigas, the trunks of matched ponderosa pines neatly hewn and darkened now by two hundred years of candle smoke. Each of these logs is supported at each end by a corbel, ornately hand carved. The ceiling of the clerestory, while higher and narrower, is similar.

The visitor is likely to notice at once that the only pews in this church are five crude benches at the sanctuary end of the nave. Ely Leyba, a villager who wrote an account of the church in 1933, explained that "during Mass, the people have learned to rest themselves by leaning against the walls of the chapel, the men on the left and the women on the right." No one seems to know why the usual pews were never installed. To the right of the entrance, a wide, low door opens from the nave into a low ceiling room. Lieutenant William Burke, surveying the territory for the U.S. Army in 1881, looked through this door and described what he saw.

"In a room to the right, which corresponds to our church

vestry, there is a hideous statue dressed in black, with a pallid face and monkish cowl, which held in its hands a bow and arrow drawn in position. 'Es la Muerte,' whispered my guide." Burke was describing Doña Sebastiana, since removed to the Penitente morada. He also described the church and its furnishings, noting wryly that the guide's statement that it had been built 130 years ago was "fully sustained by appearances." The furnishings are virtually unchanged.

The nave is decorated by two side altars, crudely made of painted planks and surmounted by religious paintings now darkened by age. There are also the traditional Stations of the Cross, scenes from the day of Christ's Crucifixion painted by an itinerant folk artist who came to Las Trampas from Sonora, Mexico, shortly after the Civil War. These are mounted in baroque frames and hung at exaggerated angles from both walls. Behind the communion rail, made of beams and painted lath, five steps lead up to the small and simple main altar which is surrounded by a similar railing. The altar screen of wood extends from floor to ceiling and features painted scenes in the Spanish folk tradition of Christ flanked by armed angels, of Saint Francis and of Saint Dominick. To the right and left are smaller side altars, one topped by a painting of Santiago on a white horse and the other by a faded representation of a crucified figure in the brown robes of a Franciscan friar. The high country is rich in the blood of such martyrs. Forty-two of the Order were slain in their attempts to Christianize the Indians, twenty-two of them in bloody 1680.

With two exceptions, the decorations of the church and its furnishings are obviously handmade. The exceptions are two round iron wood stoves which stand well out on the warped floor and are connected to the wall by stovepipe vents. In their antiquated setting, these old-fashioned heaters look incongruously modern.

Outside the church, the sun is blindingly bright, marking in a pattern of light and shadow the erosion already cut by wind and rain in the new coating of adobe on its walls. In a very few years, those who remain in Las Trampas must again mix their formula of clay and straw to repair this protective coating. Soon, when there are no longer enough Trampaseños to carry this burden, the adobe blocks of the walls will be exposed to erosion.

New Mexicans, who understand the transience of adobe structures, know how it will happen. First the roof will fall. Its leaks, left unpatched, will rot the ancient vigas until they can no longer support the weight of earthen insulation above them. The walls will last much longer. Exposed inside and out to the cycle of climate, they will collapse first above the windows and then dissolve slowly into mounds. And one day grass will grow on these mounds.

When it goes, the Church of San José de Gracia will leave no scar.

Black Jack Ketchum and the Sixteen Faithful Bartenders

The fat man on the corner stool had been talking to the bartender when I came in about how hard it was to raise turkeys because turkeys are so stupid. But he stopped and said it sure was hot and I agreed to that and he said where was I from and I said Albuquerque and he asked what brought me up to Raton and I said I'd had some business over at Folsom and he said he'd bet I knew who Sarah Rooke was then and I said as a matter of fact yes I did, she was the heroic telephone operator who got drowned in the 1908 flood and he said he'd bet I didn't know who the other sixteen people were and I admitted I didn't and then he turned back to the bartender and he said, Joe, I bet you a beer you don't know either, and the bartender said no soap.

And that fat man said, Joe, you ought to know that. Being a bartender.

Joe said well he didn't have the slightest idea.

They was all sixteen of them bartenders, the fat man said. Just like Mrs. Rooke they stayed at their posts of duty until the flood washed them all away.

It happened that I'd gone to Folsom because I was writing a magazine article about it, and therefore I had dug up all the data I could find, including the fact that its peak population was about seven hundred and its peak number of bars was seven, which comes out to one bar per one hundred residents. But seven bars divided into sixteen comes out two and two-sevenths drowned bartenders per bar.

It was a funny thing about Folsom, the fat man was saying, how determined people were, stubborn you might say. Take for example Black Jack Ketchum. Did we know about how Ketchum had found out that climbing the horseshoe curve just southeast of Folsom slowed the Colorado & Southern passenger train down so much that he could step on board right out of his stirrup without even running his horse? That Ketchum now he was one of the most ruthless badmen in the west, but he was also set in his ways, the way people get at Folsom. He robbed exactly that same train at the exact same spot three times running, and the third time, of course, the C&S railroad people had figured out the schedule and put on some guards and they wounded Ketchum and caught him and he was consequently and subsequently hanged over at Clayton with such enthusiasm that his head came off.

The bartender said he'd heard about that.

The rest of the gang got away, the fat man said. They drifted over into San Miguel and Santa Fe county and got elected to the legislature.

The fat man went back to telling stupid turkey stories and when I got back to Albuquerque I looked in the reference books. The fat man's account of Ketchum was approximately correct. I didn't find anything about the sixteen faithful bartenders but, I asked an Albuquerque barkeep about it and he said for a story like that he was prepared to apply some willing suspension of disbelief.

7

Othello in Union County

The drama was there, and a leavening of tragedy, and irony aplenty. But everything else was wrong. The affair at Folsom was out of joint with time. For example, neither of its principal characters knew the other existed. The cowboy was a book-reading, violin-playing Negro, a ranch foreman who carried a telescope in his saddle boot. The scientist collected skulls and won his highest glory for his worst mistake. It was all stranger than fiction. The one who was right about the meaning of the bone pile uncovered in Dead Horse Arroyo lies today in a weedy grave, remembered only by a few old men. But the one who was so stubbornly wrong is memorialized by a half page biography in the encyclopedia on my desk and his bust stares from a place of honor in the Smithsonian Institution.

The stage for this strangely disjointed affair was set about eleven thousand years ago. Eight miles up the valley of the Dry Cimarron from what is now the village of Folsom in Union

County, New Mexico, a band of humans trapped an unwary herd of long-horned bison. They slaughtered twenty-three of these oversize beasts, skinned them, and feasted. The carcasses lay where they had fallen. Silt gradually covered the skeletons. The light of day would not touch them again for a hundred centuries—not until August 27, 1908.

Newspapers reported that the cloudburst that afternoon dropped an incredible thirteen inches of rain on Johnson Mesa. The flood it sent roaring down the bed of the Dry Cimarron was like a tidal wave. Up the valley at the headquarters of the Crowfoot Ranch, someone heard the rumble of disaster and cranked through a warning to Sarah Rooke at her telephone switchboard in Folsom. Mrs. Rooke won a lasting place among the heroes and heroines of the Bell System by staying at her post and spreading the warning among customers until she and her office were swept away by the wall of water.

The flood washed away much of Folsom. The hunt for bodies dragged into autumn, with seventeen victims eventually recovered. Upstream, George McJunkin, the foreman of the Crowfoot, and a cowboy named Tom Wylie rode along the rim of Dead Horse Arroyo. The flood had cut its bottom much deeper than it had been. Fourteen feet down from the top of the arroyo bank, the bones of the bison slain eleven thousand years ago reflected white in the sunlight. Old bones are common in cattle country—not something to warrant a second glance from a cowboy. But George McJunkin was not the usual drover.

What we know of Nigger George McJunkin is pieced together from the little he chose to tell of his early life and from the recollections of those who knew him later. Today those memories are mixed with legend. Scholars seeking to reconstruct the man agree on some points and disagree on others. He was born a slave (or, if you prefer another version, he was the freeborn son of emancipated sharecroppers) about 1856 on an east Texas plantation owned by a man named Jack McJunkin. When the Civil War ended slavery, the boy's parents stayed on the plantation to work as sharecroppers. McJunkin befriended the boy, lent him books, and helped him learn to read. (If you prefer, his patron helped him attend school for four years. In still another version, formal education came much later, in Amarillo.) When he reached his teens, the boy headed west. At a ranch near Midland, Texas, he applied for a job and adopted his patron-landlord's name, calling himself George McJunkin. No one seems to know what his name had been before he began this new life. But apparently, unlike some former slaves, he left another name behind him.

George McJunkin is believed to have first arrived in Union County when he was twenty or twenty-one, part of a crew driving Bell Ranch cattle to summer grazing in Colorado. He got a job on a ranch near Clayton, filed a homestead claim, registered his own cattle brand, and subsequently was hired by a prominent cattleman named Bill Jack, owner of the Crowfoot, which sprawled across the Union-Colfax county border above Folsom.

A photograph taken when he was fifty-five years old shows McJunkin sitting stiffly on a large black horse. (He called his favorite mount "Headless," which made him one with Washington Irving's "Headless Horseman.") He is wearing large silver spurs, a vest, the sun frown and the faint embarrassed smile of a man posing for a camera. He is medium size, ramrod straight, slender, gray mustache trimmed, the brim of his flat-crowned felt hat turned up in front giving him a rakish look (one guesses the photographer wanted more sunlight on his face). He has the long chin and the broad, flat nose of some Negroes and he looks much younger than he must have been in 1911 when the picture was taken. Tied to the saddle behind him is a long canvas tube, too slender for a rifle scabbard. In it, George McJunkin carried the telescope through which his curious eyes surveyed the universe around him.

Three years before the picture was taken, the McJunkin curiosity had been stirred by the depth of the bones exposed in the newly cut bank of Dead Horse Arroyo. (Some call it Wild Horse Arroyo. Being cow-country-born myself, I find it easier to believe cowboys would name an arroyo, if they name it anything, after a dead horse than a wild one. Wild horses, being mobile, make poor points of reference.) McJunkin had read geology extensively and suspected that eons of silting would be required in this location to bury bones so deeply When he inspected them he saw they were too large to be the skeletons of modern buffalo—and that they were partially mineralized. He also found in what appeared to be the same stratum artifacts of chipped flint—small hide scrapers and thin, leaf-shaped points that were large for arrowheads but small for spear tips. They were nothing at all like the crude stonework with which nineteenth-century Indians littered the countryside. McJunkin's logic suggested that these bones must be immensely old, that man had killed and skinned the animals, and that therefore man must have hunted the Dry Cimarron valley many thousands of years ago. McJunkin was well enough informed of the state of anthropology to know this was exciting stuff. He set about, as best he knew how, getting the discovery to the attention of science.

Which brings us to the second actor in the drama of Folsom—Dr. Ales Hrdlicka. Hrdlicka had emigrated from Bohemia at thirteen, worked in a New York City tobacco factory, graduated from two medical colleges at the head of both classes, and won a job as coroner-medical examiner for the borough of Brooklyn. Working with the remains of the poor souls who died in public asylums, hospitals, and prisons of the city raised a question in the young physician's mind. Did these mentally deficient citizens have the same skull characteristics as the run-of-the-mill American? Hrdlicka suspected not. He began collecting the skulls of mental cases, making cranial measurements, accumulating statistics, and establishing standards. Hrdlicka seems to have accumulated and measured some two thousand skulls—a gargantuan job and a mind-boggling storage problem. And then it developed that no one had ever bothered to collect statistics on the skulls of normal persons. Thus there was no basis for comparison.

A more flexible personality might have sworn off bones for life after this debacle. Not Hrdlicka. Off to Paris he went to study bones under Dr. L. P. Manourrier, a pioneer of physical anthropology. Then to Mexico with the Lumholtz Expedition to examine the skulls of Mexican tribes. Then to the American Southwest to study American Indians for the Museum of Natural History. By 1903 Hrdlicka had established such a reputation as an authority on the skeletal structure of humankind in all its ages and varieties that the Smithsonian Institution asked him to take over its new division of physical anthropology at the National Museum. By that autumn day in 1908 when Nigger George McJunkin was finding his bison bones, Ales Hrdlicka had published the first of his major books, *Psychological and Medical Observations among the Indians of the Southwestern States and Northern Mexico*. More significant, Hrdlicka had also published his first important paper attacking a claim to antiquity for an anthropological discovery.

The so-called Calaveras Skull (found 130 feet beneath a glacial gravel bed in California) could not be as old as its location suggested, Hrdlicka reported, because its bone structure was clearly modern. Hrdlicka proved to be correct. Calaveras was exposed as an elaborate hoax. The young bone specialist was already assuming the role of defender of scientific accuracy. The times demanded just such a man.

Only fifty years had passed since discovery of fist axes in European glacial deposits had first suggested that man had been around the planet a lot longer than the six thousand years allowed by accepted Calvinistic philosophy. Quite a lot had been learned subsequently about the development of *homo sapiens* from the primates. The beetle-browed skull of Neanderthal Man had been dug out of his cave in Germany and was now turning up throughout the Middle East and Asia. The great blank spots in the history of man's first million years were filling fast. Scientific circles buzzed with new finds, new theories, and with hoaxes and humbug, bad guesses and crackpot speculation. (A pictograph of a lizard found in Arizona was used as proof that man was contemporaneous with the dinosaur in America.) From such chaos, Hrdlicka and other like-minded scientists were beginning to bring a cautious order. As curator of physical anthropology of the National Museum and founding editor of the *Journal of Physical Anthropology,* Hrdlicka was in the right place for the job. He became America's last word on the antiquity of human bone. By the time McJunkin was making serious efforts to lure scientists to Folsom to take a look at Dead Horse Arroyo, Hrdlicka and associates had sorted through the nonsense and hysteria to a bedrock of common sense. In brief, they concluded that what McJunkin thought had happened in New Mexico was impossible. There had been no Ice Age Man in America.

It seemed clear enough. There had been no primates in the Western Hemisphere. Therefore men could not have evolved here. The only possible route for aboriginal man (lacking seacraft) to reach this hemisphere would be out of Siberia across the Bering Straits. Hrdlicka's own pioneering research established definite links between people in Central Asia and the American Indians. But these Mongoloid people could not have crossed the straits into Alaska while the route was blocked by the great, slow-melting ice cap of the Wisconsin glaciation. There had been no ice-free passages until about three thousand to four thousand years ago. Supporting this late-arrival theory was negative evidence. Hrdlicka had established to his own satisfaction that Neanderthal Man had evolved into a man with a modern skull shape only about six thousand years ago. All human bones found in the New World were modern bones. There were none of those big-toothed skulls with the bony ridges over the eye sockets so common in the Old World. Therefore ancient man had not reached the Americas.

The only fault you can find with Hrdlicka's theory is that it was wrong. Neanderthal did not evolve into modern man. The modern skull type developed at least forty thousand years ago and probably much earlier than that. And ice-free passages across from Asia seem to have come and gone many thousands of years back into prehistory.

As curator of physical anthropology at the National Museum, Hrdlicka stood like Horatio at the bridge, defending anthropological truth against the besieging army of error (or perhaps even deceit). As his stature and reputation grew and his fame became international, any discovery involving human antiquity in the Americas had to get past the sharp and suspicious eyes of his National Museum staff to be certified as legitimate. Thus the word which filtered out of New Mexico of a site where human tools were mixed with Ice Age animal bones met skepticism. George McJunkin might have just as well been trying to sell a dragon. No one was interested enough to come and look.

Nor was the Folsom site the only victim. In 1914, human bones were found with the bones of ground sloth and other extinct mammals not far from Los Angeles. In 1916, human bones and stone tools were discovered with mastodon and mammoth remains deep under the earth at Vero Beach and Melbourne, Florida. In each case, and in a good many others, Hrdlicka's forces held the bridge. The bones were ruled modern and the circumstances explained away. Perhaps, it was said, they had been dumped into a grave dug down into the fossil deposit, or perhaps erosion had mixed the artifacts into the mastodon skeletons, or perhaps roots growing downward had pushed the stone tools down among the bones. The evidence seems to have been inspected with the same sort of enthusiasm a virologist would show for arguments that toads cause warts.

Among the discoveries debunked by Hrdlicka happened to be one made by Jesse Figgins of the Colorado Museum of Natural History (now the Denver Museum). Hrdlicka was not the sort to spare the feelings of the recipients of his unfavorable rulings and the records suggest that Figgins was determined not to lose a second argument with the man at the Smithsonian. When he ordered the bones recovered from Dead Horse Arroyo he warned the digging crew to be especially alert for human artifacts which might be found among the fossils. If any were found every precaution would be taken to preserve the evidence. It was spring, 1926. In Washington, Hrdlicka was at work on his sixth major book, which would be a college text and would support Hrdlicka's point that the First Americans had migrated to the New World only recently from Asia. And in Folsom, Nigger George McJunkin had gone to his grave in the village cemetery.

For McJunkin the last years must have been disappointing. In 1918, the Jacks had sold the Crowfoot to the Lud Shoemaker family. McJunkins stayed on as foreman and that same year he and the Shoemaker's teen-age son, Ivan, dug more bones and a fluted lance point out of the arroyo bank and got them off to the Denver Museum. The next spring the museum sent a paleontologist named Harold J. Cook to the Crowfoot, where McJunkin helped him with some exploratory digging. At last science was interested.

But nothing happened, and 1920 came and went without a word. In 1921, McJunkin fell ill. By summer he was often too weak to ride. By fall he moved his belongings into the lean-to room at the rear of the Folsom Hotel. There was little enough to move. His house on the Crowfoot had been struck by lightning and burned, destroying his telescope, his violin, his well-read books, and a lifetime's collection of fossils, oddities, and artifacts. The doctor came to Folsom to examine him. He proclaimed his disease to be incurable dropsy. Whiskey seemed to ease the pain. A cowboy friend rigged up a system of rubber tubing which allowed him to sip from his bottle. When he became too weak to hold a book, young Ivan Shoemaker would read to him—often from the Old Testament. The way Shoemaker recalls it, McJunkin died on a cold, dark night in March 1922, telling those keeping the death watch with him that he was "going where all good niggers go."

(The man waiting in the Doherty Mercantile Store, which now serves as the Folsom Museum, had heard about it from his daddy and he knew George McJunkin only by local legend. "They didn't know his real name. Not even to put it on his grave marker," the man said. "That always seemed sort of sad to me.")

To me, many things about the life of Nigger George McJunkin seem sort of sad. Even with today's all-weather highways, the world of the Dry Cimarron remains a closed world. Johnson Mesa walls it off from the Colorado to the north. In all other directions the barrier is space—that rolling sea of grass that is the western fringe of the Great Plains. Once this was Comanche country. But when McJunkin arrived it was white man country. For most of his adult life he was the only black man in it. The legend does not tell us that his race isolated him. But Ivan Shoemaker remembers two stories McJunkin liked to tell in his declining years. In one a cattle drover friend pulls his pistol in the lobby of the Eklund Hotel in Clayton to persuade the manager he should serve Nigger George in the hotel dining room. In another, the cowboys from the Crowfoot—at a neighboring ranch to help brand the spring calf crop—walk out when they learn Nigger George is being segregated into the kitchen for his lunch. The stories seem to tell us that this man with his flat nose and his black skin was included in the fraternity of the west. But don't they tell us that only part—and perhaps a very small part—of this society accepted him as an equal? His pride in them is revealing.

We also know that Nigger George became the unofficial surveyor and arbitrator of property disputes in that big empty country. Such an assignment shows the community acknowledged his skill and his fairness. It also suggests something less comfortable. The arbiter cannot be friend to either side. It is the thankless job which rural society reserves for the outsider.

If his race hadn't made him that, it seems to me his turn of intellect would have done it. The flintiness of life at the turn of the century on the windy east slope of the Rocky Mountains demanded concentration on the essentials—the market, the feed supply, the desperate need for rain, the gynecology of cattle. There was no time for philosophy, or abstractions, or books, and scanty interest. The bison bones McJunkin put on his mantel and his habit of talking about them produced amusement among his neighbors. Fossil bones were no more useful than the constellations which McJunkin studied through his telescope. A hungry land held little patience for the hungry mind. Nigger George in Union County recalls Othello among the Venetians, misfit more by mind than by color. He was a stranger in a strange land.

Had he lived to see it, McJunkin would have been immensely pleased by the Dead Horse Arroyo dig. Fairly early the crew from Denver knew the find was important. The skeletons were still articulated, which meant the deposit had not been disturbed by erosion or anything else. And among the bones in the hard clay were artifacts made by man. Figgins and Cook contacted archaeologists and anthropologists and tried to persuade them that these extinct animals had been killed by man. They failed. The anthropologists argued that the artifacts might have somehow worked down into the deposit.

Four times, when the dig resumed in the summer of 1927, projectile points were noticed only after they had been jarred loose from the clay holding the bones. The fifth point was noticed in time. Figgins stopped work and sent telegrams. Frank H. H. Roberts of the Smithsonian, Barnum Brown of the American Museum of Natural History, and A. V. Kidder of Phillips Academy arrived, studied the lance point embedded between two ribs, and agreed that The-Man-Who-Could-Not-Be had, in fact, been.

Figgins and Cook published their report in *Natural History,* announcing what they had found. Science generally remained skeptical. Figgins ordered the dig continued into the third summer. This time the American Museum of Natural History joined the expedition. Again points were found among the bones. One had been jammed between two vertebrae and snapped off. The broken butt was found and matched with the tip. And there was more proof now. It dawned on Barnum Brown that the tailbones were missing from all twenty-three skeletons because, as they say in cow country, "The tail goes with the hide." The bison had all been skinned. Some of the bones also showed the marks left by flint knives cutting away the flesh. Some had been cooked. Again telegrams were sent to the doubters.

At the very moment when Figgins and crew were reducing his theory to nonsense, Hrdlicka was publishing a broadside blast which should have sunk, once and for all, the persistent idea of Early Man in America. *Scientific American,* then as now the prestige interdiscipline magazine of science, gave him its cover and devoted most of an edition to a long and profusely illustrated article by Hrdlicka. It bore the unflinching, unqualified subtitle: THERE IS NO VALID EVIDENCE THAT THE INDIAN HAS LONG BEEN IN THE NEW WORLD.

Even when read today, with full knowledge of how wrong he was, the brilliant Czech's arguments are almost persuasive. Hrdlicka wrote in an era before anthropology fell into the turgid, semiliterate jargon it uses today. His prose is graceful, his thesis lucid, and his case for an America populated from Asia no earlier than a couple of thousand years ago seems ironclad. And then, almost as if fate had conspired for the scientific establishment to disgrace itself, it was announced that Hrdlicka had been invited to London, there to address the Royal Academy. The Royal Anthropological Society, to anthropology what the College of Cardinals is to the Vatican, would call itself into a rare special meeting to hear Hrdlicka lecture. And it would award him the Huxley Medal. This signal honor would be in recognition of his years of service in destroying "unwarranted claims for the extreme antiquity of man in America."

By 1930 and 1931 field anthropologists almost universally accepted the reality of the strange hunter whom Figgins called "Folsom Man" (the village, fortunately, had changed its name from Ragtown much earlier). By 1934, Hrdlicka's own Smithsonian people were excavating the great Lindenmeier Ranch site in Colorado and the horizon of man in the Western Hemisphere was being pushed still further back by discovery of a mammoth hunter near Clovis, New Mexico. Hrdlicka was swept aside. He could do no more than stalk angrily from a session of the American Anthropological Association when a report on Early Man was being read.

An incident has rarely been less kind to those who influenced

it. Folsom came too late for George McJunkin. It came too early
for Ales Hrdlicka. He lived on, seeing his books turn from dogma
to bad guesses and his theories shattered by discovery after discovery. His last book was an odd work entitled *Children Who Run
on All Fours,* which appeared in 1931. In 1942 he retired as curator
of the division of physical anthropology, leaving it its superb
skeletal collections and its bright worldwide reputation. He died
the next year.

I know Ales Hrdlicka only in the least satisfactory of ways—
having tracked his ghost in the archives of libraries, seeking a
personality in what he wrote. What I think I saw between the
lines in those outdated journals was a man of tremendous en-
ergy, self-discipline, almost arrogant self-esteem, and unusual
intelligence. I think he would have little tolerance of me, or of
you (who are at this very moment wasting precious time), or of
George McJunkin.

Perhaps because I sense this, I find I enjoy standing by the
vast old wood stove at the rear of the Doherty Mercantile Store
and thinking perverse anti-intellectual thoughts. For seventeen
years the drovers and gandy dancers who thawed their boots
here and heard Nigger George speculate on the meaning of the
Dead Horse Arroyo bones had a clearer idea of the prehistory of
their continent than did all the certified brains of the Department of Physical Anthropology of the National Museum. It's an
unkind thought but if it does Dr. Hrdlicka injustice it can do him
no harm.

The Committee and the Mule Deer

It was one of those winter days which residents of the Rocky Mountains remember with fierce nostalgia when exiled to the flatlands. At this elevation, five hundred feet above the seven-thousand-foot altitude of the Santa Fe plaza, the air was cold but the sun beat down from a dark blue sky. There was no wind, no dust, no humidity, the sort of day when skiers doff their jackets and come home at dusk with both frostbite and sunburn. Thirty miles northwestward across the Rio Grande Valley, Los Alamos was etched white against the Ponderosa green of the Jemez Mountains. Sixty miles south the snow-rimmed hump of Sandia Mountain looked close enough to touch. The air had that odd, intense clarity peculiar to the mountain country on cold, cloudless, dry days.

The site selection committee from St. John's College stood under this mountain sun, bundled against the drearier winter of

Maryland's humid tidewater climate, and looked around. They were on a high slope of a Sangre de Cristo foothill which locals call Moonmount. They hadn't originally planned to be here. They had been en route to Claremont, California, to inspect a tract of land on which their ancient Annapolis liberal arts college would probably build its new western campus. There, St. John's would become part of the famous "Claremont cluster" —sharing library, laboratory, and other facilities with Pomona, Scripps, and Claremont colleges. The advantages of the California site were numerous and obvious. The stop-off of these professors in New Mexico to view land offered there was mostly a matter of courtesy. So today the committee was among the piñons on the side of Moonmount, walking now on places where the sun had evaporated the snow.

Years have passed and I forget their names and even their number—five, I would guess, but perhaps as many as seven, generally young, made pale by the weak sun of the coastal climate and their scholarly profession, generally urban, generally Eastern, solidly W.A.S.P. They came from a world which was old Anglo-Saxon family, old books, Greek and Latin literacy, prep schools and bluepoint oysters and Ivy League; a world bounded on the north by Boston (or perhaps Vermont) and on the south by Virginia, in which the West consisted of San Francisco, reached on airliner flights over an American interior as vacant as the Australian outback. None of them, unless my memory fails me, had visited the Southern Rockies before this day. It seemed to me that for this group the landscape around them and the culture of the Rio Arriba was stranger than the Lake District of Britain or the Aegean Islands. This was the country of the most vulgar American mythology, of cowboy and Indian, raw material only for children's literature. Northing here of particular interest to mainstream scholarship.

One of them, a youngish, slightly skinny man who might have been a professor of Romance languages, had stopped at a place where trees and the slant of ground protected a field of snow from the sun. Not many hours earlier a single deer had strolled across this expanse and the professor had noticed the tracks. In a moment, his fellow tutors were standing beside him examining the hoofprints.

"Are those deer tracks?" the professor asked. "They are, aren't they?"

"A mule deer," said one of the local guides, and noticing the interest, he squatted by the snow for a closer look. "An old buck," he said. "See how big the track is, and how it's splayed, and how the front of the back hooves are rounded off. They do that by dragging their feet when they're rutting."

The group stood around the snow patch while the Santa Fean explained something of the solitary grouchiness of elderly male mule deer, and identified other tracks in the snow—the drag marks of a procupine and the footprints of assorted birds.

The committee left the next day for Claremont, and then flew back to Annapolis where the members recommended, without dissent, that the western campus of St. John's be located at Santa Fe, New Mexico. I understand no mention was made of deer tracks.

8

Quijote in Rio Arriba County

When Doyle Akers, chief of the Rio Arriba County bureau of *The New Mexican,* drove his pickup truck into Tierra Amarilla on June 5, 1967, he was puzzled. At the edge of town he had met the patrol car of Deputy Sheriff Pete Jaramillo. Akers had pulled to the side of the road, expecting the lawman to stop to exchange news, as was their custom. But the patrol car drove slowly past and the man driving it was not Jaramillo. He was a younger man wearing a red beret.

Akers did not see his friend Jaramillo sitting on the passenger side—attempting to signal him by shaking his head in a vigorous negative. Jaramillo's arms were handcuffed behind his back and the man in the beret held a .38-caliber pistol cocked against his side. In the back seat, a United Press International reporter sat guarded by a man holding a military model .30-caliber carbine.

In a moment Akers forgot the question of who was driving

the deputy's car in a stranger puzzle. He noticed first that the streets of the shabby little town of five hundred people were utterly and eerily deserted, and next that two State Police cars parked by the courthouse were riddled with bullet holes. He walked toward the silent courthouse, noticing a bullet hole through the window of the sheriff's office and another through one of the building's double front doors, noticing that the redness splashed on the front steps was blood, not yet dried.

The courthouse lobby was empty. Here, too, there was blood—a smear of it under the county bulletin board and more on the floor by the telephone booth. The telephone had been jerked from the wall and the glass shattered by a bullet. Through the floor of the sheriff's office, Akers could see that the county's radio transmitter had been smashed and scattered across the door. The hallway around him was littered with spent pistol and carbine cartridges. He saw more blood on the stairs leading to the courtroom on the second floor and that the courtroom doors had been broken open. He walked down the hall toward the County Commission meeting room. As he reached the door, it opened. Sheriff Benny Naranjo stuck out his head. The sheriff's shirt was dappled with blood. Behind him in the meeting room, Akers saw some twenty men and women—most of them county officials and courthouse employees.

"Are they gone?" Naranjo asked.

"They" were a platoon of about twenty armed men—the "arresting party" of an organization that called itself the Alianza Federal de Mercedes and that denied the jurisdiction of the United States over millions of acres of territory in the Southwest. This band had captured the courthouse of Rio Arriba County, New Mexico, in a lightning raid two hours earlier, shooting or clubbing five state and county lawmen and holding most of the building's occupants as prisoners. The raiders had left moments before Akers arrived, taking two hostages and leaving a wreckage of shattered windows, broken doors, demolished communications equipment, and ransacked county records.

Incredible as it seems, the raid on Tierra Amarilla represented neither a single act of banditry nor the spontaneous violence of a mob. It was a carefully planned effort to capture the District Attorney of New Mexico's First Judicial District and bring him to trial in a court of the Pueblo Republic of San Joaquín. The raiders had been picked for this assignment by the Department of Vigilance of this self-proclaimed "city-state." They included small farmers, sheepherders, and common laborers, a newly wed husband, a great-grandfather, and a teen-age boy. Their common denominator was poverty, a share in New Mexico's sour heritage of Spanish land grants, and a belief in the sometimes angry but always eloquent message of a man named Reies Lopez Tijerina. He was a man whom many of New Mexico's Anglo-Americans found difficult to understand. But then most of them probably hadn't read Miguel Cervantes's account of the man from La Mancha who dreamed of glory, honor, and justice. New-Mexico Hispanos, their roots in the past of Cervantes's Spain, understood Tijerina perfectly.

Tijerina had founded his Alianza in 1963. Its charter states that its cause is to "organize grants covered by the Guadalupe-Hidalgo Treaty . . . thus providing unity of purpose and securing for the heirs of Spanish Land Grants the highest advantages as provided therein." The words sound mild, but only until the history of these grants is considered.

When the United States Senate ratified the Treaty of Guadalupe Hidalgo in 1848 and took the Territories of New Mexico and Northern California from the defeated Republic of Mexico, the land grants totaled an estimated thirty-three million acres. There were more than a thousand of them, mostly made in the names of the kings of Spain by the royal viceroys in Mexico City. Some were issued to individuals by name, but most were "communal" grants. In these, individual settlers were given title in their own name to very small tracts at the community village and shared equal communal rights with all other settlers to use the water, grazing, and timber throughout the land grant. Under the Spanish system, the settlers were guaranteed that these community rights would continue through their descendants *por siempre*. In England, *por siempre* means "forever." But forever proved remarkably brief. This utopian *ejido* system of King Charles V left in its wake, as the Spanish empire receded and collapsed, a legacy of trouble. From Argentina to Mexico it produced a history of land seizure, exploitation, and combat and made "land reform" the banner of a hundred bloody revolutions. Nuevo Mexico, the northernmost fringe of the colonies of Spain, was not to escape this grim inheritance.

In the first years of American occupation, U.S. military commanders notified the new citizens that only "quiet possession" of the grants would be needed to prove ownership. But the government decided otherwise. It required that all claims to lands be registered with the Federal Land Office. Clear documentary proof would be needed to establish ownership. Otherwise the land would be placed in the public domain as federal property.

In many cases, the villagers—illiterate and utterly ignorant of the American legal system—lost all rights to their ancestral lands before they knew these rules existed. For most of them, a generation would pass before they were aware that the law had made them squatters in their family homes. Since no one else wanted the land, they continued to occupy it as they had for two hundred years, growing subsistence crops where there was no water to irrigate and grazing their small herds on grass no one else had use for. As late as 1870 nothing much had changed. But in 1870, time was running out for the Spanish Americans.

That year the first property tax law went into effect in New Mexico Territory—a law which would put the land of thousands of moneyless Spanish families on the sheriff's auction block. The same year, a room in the territorial capitol building was cleaned out to provide space for a new attorney general. Dusty old papers, stacked to the ceiling, were given to convicts to be hauled away as scrap. Weeks passed before horrified New Mexicans learned that waste paper now kindling fireplaces was the Spanish and Mexican territorial archives. The only documentary hope of many land grant farmers of proving ownership of their land was scattered to the winds.

While these incidents at home were damaging, disaster came from the East. The railroads moved toward New Mexico, opening the land. Simultaneously, the price of beef, mutton, and wool skyrocketed. Suddenly the land and grass which no one else wanted were in immense demand. The 57,000 cattle and 600,000 sheep counted in the territory in 1870 became 1,600,000 cows and some 4,000,000 sheep in the 1880s. In a single generation of frantic range-grabbing and land speculation, the colonists of New Mexico lost what their forefathers had held since the seventeenth century.

It happened in many ways. In some cases, it was a brutally simple seizure of land by the armed riders of the cattle companies. But generally a shadowy organization known to historians as "The Santa Fe Ring" was involved and the piracy was more sophisticated. Sometimes it was even legal.

The Ring included leaders in both Republican and Democratic parties and key men in the Federal Land Office and the U.S. Office of Surveyor General. It controlled the legislature, law enforcement, and the courts, and had powerful influence in Washington. Its methods were efficient.

The Maxwell Land Grant is a case in point. When Ring members obtained this grant it included 96,000 acres. The federal surveyor– also in the Ring—redrew the boundaries to include 1,760,000 acres. The territorial governor, another creature of the organization, authorized a notorious Colorado killer and gambler to organize a "militia" of hired gunmen to evict the farmers who had owned the land before this fraudulent survey. When the settlers tried to fight back, he issued an official proclamation making it illegal for them to bear arms.

Elsewhere methods were devised to fit the situation. In western New Mexico a 240-square-mile empire of grass was seized by filing a string of fraudulent homestead claims in the Ring-controlled land office, thus cutting the other users off from all water supplies. Some settlers resisted and became the victims of what history calls "The American Valley Murders." In Rio Arriba County, the huge Tierra Amarilla Land Grant was captured by buying rights from a single villager and then filing a patented title claiming the entire communal holdings. Often even the small holdings didn't escape this plunder. When farmers learned they had no title to their family land and came to the land office to file a homestead claim as allowed by American law, it was common practice for corrupt officials to write out a false land description. The illiterate farmer would sign this, falsely certifying in his ignorance that he was living on land somewhere else. The official would then file another homestead claim on the farmer's land in the name of a confederate. If the victim objected, he would be shown his signature on the false claim and threatened with arrest and prosecution.

By the turn of the century, one man—a former Confederate artillery officer named Thomas B. Catron—held title to more than two million acres in New Mexico and held an interest in millions more—controlling an expanse almost as large as Massachusetts. Of the 33 million acres in Spanish grants, all but 1.9 million had vanished into national forests or public domain—and from the public domain through land frauds into the hands of the cattle companies.

Virtually all of the remaining grants had fallen into Anglo-American hands. Instead of their ancestral lands, the twentieth-century descendants of the Trujillos, Garcías, and Bacas inherited their grandfathers' stories of how those lands were stolen. Virtually every family has such a story—a folklore of injustice, helpless humiliation, and sometimes violence. In the villages of mountainous northern New Mexico, the loss of the land grants made poverty both inevitable and incurable. Poor men, surrounded by the grass and timber of their stolen heritage, find these stories of injustice hard to forget. And to these men, Reies Lopez Tijerina began preaching the message of his Alianza in 1963.

The press in New Mexico sometimes called Tijerina "The King Tiger." When one considered the man and not his violent effect the title seemed incongruous. He is a slender, average-size man and his forehead bears the fatigue lines of the average man in his early forties. But his eyes are not average. A striking hazel-green under heavy black eyebrows, they light his face with an alert, and curiously happy, intelligence.

One also noticed, when talking to Tijerina of his Alianza movement, that he was not troubled by doubts of either his abilities or the rightness of what he was doing. He was infinitely self-assured. He is also a handsome man, and aware of it. It is a product, he said, of the Indian blood in the family. He said it without vanity, simply listing an asset which balances liabilities about which he was equally frank—nervousness, a quick, hot temper, and an imperfect command of English phraseology. Just as simply, he listed another asset.

"I am not a man who is afraid," he said. For one who had chosen social revolution as his mission, it was a necessary attribute. And not even his bitter enemies denied the statement.

Tijerina was born in 1927 in a one-room sharecropper shack near Falls City, Texas, the son of Antonio and Herlinda Tijerina. He had four brothers and two sisters. Three other children of the family were victims of the notoriously high infant mortality rate of migrant workers. Like those who were to follow him, Tijerina's only inheritance was abject poverty and a handed-down family story of injustice at the hands of Anglo Americans. His great-grandfather was a horse breeder who owned grant land north of Laredo, Texas. When Anglo ranchers wanted the land, Tijerina says, they drove branded cattle into one of his corrals and accused him of stealing them. "And then six Texas Rangers came and hanged him from a tree in his own yard."

"My grandfather, Santiago Tijerina, was a boy then. He stood there and watched that hanging and it put bitterness in him," Tijerina explained. "Later on he dealt some in contraband and once they hanged him, too, but they decided they had the wrong man and they cut him down before he strangled."

The bitterness put into Santiago Tijerina as a boy was enough to last him a lifetime. When he was dying he called his grandson from a job in Michigan to his deathbed, and spent his last two days recalling the days of dispossession, brutality, injustice, outrage, and indignity his family had suffered. "He was seventy-eight then, but he could still show me the rope scars the noose had left around his neck," Tijerina recalled.

Tijerina talked of his grandfather with nostalgic fondness, describing him as a "lion of a man—a man they could never break." He talked of his mother, who died when he was seven, with warmth, and the stories he told made you suspect he might have been her favorite. But he talked of his father reluctantly.

"He was timid," Tijerina said. "We were sharecroppers. You work somebody's farm and get a share of the crop. But three times, *three different times,* when we got the crop laid by they would come and tell my father to pack up and get out. And my father put us children and our stuff in the wagon and we got out without getting anything for our work." As Tijerina told this, he looked at you as if hoping you could explain the conundrum of avarice and despair.

"Three times it happened. And the last time—I remember it better because I was older—we were working for a man named Albert and his three boys came one day on their horses and they tried to rope my dad with a lasso. He couldn't get around good because one of his legs was crippled. They told him to get off the place. That time my father went into town and told the sheriff about it."

Tijerina smiled at this memory. And, incredibly, the smile seemed neither ironic nor bitter. He seemed as genuinely amused at this evidence of his father's innocence as he was baffled by what he called his father's "trembling." It would take a weaker man than Reies Tijerina (or Don Quijote) to understand fear.

"The sheriff said, 'Tony, that Mr. Albert's no better than an outlaw and I can't do anything with him. If he finds out you came here and told on him, he won't even let you get your chickens off his place.' So we went back and got those chickens and after that we moved to San Antonio."

In San Antonio, the twelve-year-old Tijerina enrolled in school for the first time and began learning English. (He is still studying it. "Which is it?" he asked. "Should I say 'figuratively' or 'symbolically'?") The family was working as migrant farm labor and there was time for only a few months of schooling, but Tijerina learned to read seventh-grade books.

In 1949, he enrolled in the Assemblies of God Church School at Ysleta, Texas, to study evangelism. He is remembered by those who taught him as a sincere, reform-conscious student and as a fiery and effective preacher with sometimes unorthodox views. The fundamentalist religious group sent Tijerina to Santa Fe, New Mexico, to help at a revival. In New Mexico these "unorthodox views" caused the church to cancel his credentials. The twenty-three-year-old preacher, now on his own, spent months on and around the Tierra Amarilla Land Grant trying to organize a religious sect and, as he remembers it, "talking to the old people and learning about what happened to their land."

Thirteen years passed before Tijerina would use that knowledge. He wandered, working as a farm laborer, through the Midwest and finally settled in Arizona in 1957. Near Casa Grande, he and seventeen other migrant workers bought land, built homes for their families, and erected a small chapel.

"We elected trustees and called it 'Valle de Paz,' our valley of peace." He grinned. "That turned out to be ironic because the people around there didn't want us as neighbors. There was harassment—mostly just teen-agers who would come when we were all away working in the cotton fields. But they burned down my house and in two years they had burned down everything."

Arizona records show that during this period Tijerina and three others living at what police accounts describe as a "gypsy camp" were charged with stealing tires from a trailer. Before this charge was dropped for lack of evidence, Tijerina was arrested again—this time charged with attempting to free his brother, Margarito, from jail. During his trial on this charge, Tijerina walked away from the courthouse during a noon recess and vanished. He left his burned-out Valley of Peace and prepared for a more warlike mission. He had, he explained, a very strange dream.

"I was sleeping on the ground in cold weather and I saw a landscape with tall pines and the walls of an old kingdom. There were horses standing there, frozen. But they began melting and coming to life again. I knew it was New Mexico because of the pines and the old walls and when I got to Mexico City, I found the land grants were like those horses—not dead but frozen."

(Tijerina sometimes tells of two other dreams. One is a boyhood nightmare, the sight of the landlord's Ford rolling, driverless, toward the Tijerina shack and the knowledge that one of the family will be killed for stealing it. The other seems to him more like a vision. It happened when he was four; a dream of a flower garden and in it Jesus pulling him in a red wagon. Remembering it, he smiles ruefully. "I never did get to ride in a red wagon," he says.)

Tijerina spent much of the next six years in Mexico "doing research into the laws of the Spanish Empire and the background of the land grants." Then the voice of the Tiger began being heard in northern New Mexico.

The message was clear. Join the Alianza Federal de Mercedes. It would restore the birthright of the disinherited Spanish Americans. How? The land grants, Tijerina explained, were based on the authority of the Spanish crown. The Mexicans had no right to cede this land to the United States. It was necessary only for the land grant heirs to unite and to assert their independence from the United States and their rights to the grants. With this call for action, Tijerina taught his philosophy. The Spanish Americans, he argued, were neither Spanish nor Americans. They were a new race which dated from October 19, 1541, when the Spanish government decreed the legality of intermarriage between Spanish colonists and the Indians. As a new race they were immature. They could not compete with the Anglo Caucasians—a race with the wisdom and strength of thousands of years. In the Anglo culture based on materialism, they were no better than children. They should unite, recover their ancestral lands, set up their own society, and live in peace and dignity.

Don Quijote de la Mancha armed himself with a rusty lance when he set forth on his spavined horse to turn back the clock in Renaissance Spain—and his dream was simple. Quijote would restore the age of chivalry and with it brotherhood, decency, honor, and even glory to a degraded humanity. Tijerina armed himself with mimeographed copies of the Treaty of Guadalupe Hidalgo and quotations from the *Recompilation of the Laws of the Indies* issued in 1570 by Philip II. His dream, too, was simple. He would unite the dispossessed Hispano heirs to the land grants, reclaim their land, and set up a separate kingdom. If completely realized, Tijerina's goal involved overturning ownership of much of the most valuable land from Texas to the Pacific, property worth billions of dollars. It involved successful seccession from the United States of 1,715 independent land grant states scattered through the American Southwest. If Quijote's vision was "the impossible dream," Tijerina's seemed downright incredible.

He covered the state in his old car, concentrating on the north, speaking to any group that would listen to him. He was an eloquent man speaking to people who understood and valued eloquence. More than that. When Tijerina spoke it was apparent to even the most wary and cynical that he *believed*. Every word rang with this furious, fanatic faith. "They have stolen your land and given you welfare. They took the grass where you grazed your cattle and they give you powdered milk. They rob your children of our language and rob us all of our manhood and tell us we are no-good Mexicans, cowards, lazy, worthless. But the land is ours. The documents prove it. Justice is with us. Law is with us. God is with us. We are members of the Holy Race, Hidalgos."

He would read from the treaty the promise of the United States of America to honor and protect the property rights of Mexicans. He would remind his audience that the Indians had recovered their land. He would offer hope where there hadn't been hope for a full generation.

This message had little appeal to better educated, more sophisticated Spanish Americans—the majority which competes successfully in New Mexico politics, business, and the professions. But among the villages of the mountain counties, and among refugees from these dying communities, the tone of the Tijerina appeal struck a responsive chord. It offered hope.

In Rio Arriba County, the unemployment rate of the mid-1960s was 20.2 percent—six times the national average and double the rate of the Negro slums of Watts and Harlem. Among the Spanish Americans who make up 70 percent of the county's population the rate of joblessness was closer to 30 percent. In Kentucky's depression-ridden Appalachia region, which had drawn national attention and massive federal aid, 30 percent of the families live below the "poverty line" of $3,000 annual income. But in New Mexico's forgotten mountain poverty pockets, 48.8 percent live on less than $3,000 family income, and in Rio Arriba County 37 percent of the families exist with annual incomes under $2,000. In the old land grant country the infant mortality rate is two and one-half times the national average and deaths by diarrhea, the telltale index of unsanitary conditions, are ten times national levels. Grim as they are, such statistics tell only part of the story.

Much more than the decaying city ghetto, the dying mountain communities have trapped their occupants. The villager is trapped in part because he doesn't want to leave. Here he has dignity. His ancestors named the mountains, the streams, and the mesas that surround him. Here he is known and respected. His children are among aunts and cousins, encompassed by the care and affection of the Spanish "extended family." Here he can at least grow a few beans and chile peppers and, since mud adobe bricks cost nothing, have his own walls around him. If he could escape to the slums of the city all this would be lost, and with it his identity.

But for many there is no escape even when hunger forces them to try. In Rio Arriba County in the 1960s almost half of those over twenty-five had only a grade school education. In Taos County, 25 percent of the adults had completed no more than the fourth grade. Many speak little or no English. In New Mexico's science-oriented economy, there is no place for the un-educated and unskilled.

Among those trapped in this chronic poverty Reies Tijerina found most of his followers. His recruiting was helped by a long accumulation of specific frustrations—with rutted roads impass-able in the winter, with village schools closed in consolidation programs, and with years of broken political promises. But the United States Forest Service helped most of all. Under policies aimed at improving range management and developing more ef-ficient use of national timberlands, the Forest Service began en-forcing old rules with new efficiency.

The old practice that allowed families to pasture a milk cow and a team of plow horses in the forest without owning a graz-ing allotment was ended. It was a small thing, but not for the man left without milk for his children and with no way to plow his fields. Villagers with grazing permits had other troubles. The agency began imposing cash trespass fines against farmers whose cows drifted off allotted areas. It cut the grazing season—in some cases from nine months to five. It required fencing that many could not afford to buy. It began forcing the periodic move-ment of cattle from one range to another—a conservation move practical for the cattle companies with hired cowboys but hard indeed for a farmer who must leave his few cows and his village for the summer to work in the Colorado beet fields and herd sheep in Montana.

The Forest Service denies any sinister intention behind these range-improving policies. But the villagers hear of 2,000 cattle being grazed by a cattle company in a national forest to the south, of a family with a permit for 450 head, and of a Colorado rancher running 200 cattle in their village forest. Some of them believe the Forest Service is deliberately trying to harass the small permit holder off the range to make room for the big operators. Those who believe this listen when the Alianza tells them that the forest taken from their grandfathers can be theirs again if they will take it back.

More than thirty families around El Rito joined the Alianza en masse after being told they must build fences dividing their Forest Service allotments. Others joined after petitioning Congress to investigate Forest Service policies and seeing their request ignored. Dozens of families around Regina joined after a rural school was closed. Others began paying the dues—one dollar per month per family—after they failed again for the fifteenth consecutive year to get gravel put on the rutted mud of their children's schoolbus route.

Just how many heard the Alianza's promises and signed as members is a matter of controversy. Tijerina claimed thirty thousand and federal officials guessed about five thousand. Whatever the number, Tijerina seems to have decided in the autumn of 1966 that his organization was strong enough to turn from oratory to action.

The strategy of Reies Tijerina was simple and predoomed.

He hoped to force the federal government into a confrontation in a court of law, and specifically to place on the United States the burden of proving its rights to former land grants. He believed the government had no such legal proof and that the Alianza would triumph. To force this confrontation, the Alianza would concentrate its force and seize a single land grant.

The San Joaquín grant, issued in 1806 in the rugged Rio Chama canyon, was picked. Its location was ideal—in an area where poverty was extreme and Alianza membership correspondingly high. More important, nearly all of the land to be claimed lay in the Carson National Forest, with few private owners to be offended. However, since Tijerina was hoping to force a confrontation in court test of fundamental ownership rights, the grant had the fatal flaw of being mostly phony. The records of the Land Claims Commission show it was originally—like most late grants—very small. It had been bought by the Santa Fe Ring, and its margins inflated from some 2,000 acres to about 600,000. But the fraud had been too obvious and the claim had been rejected. Such details matter only if one deals with windmills as windmills and not when he calls them giants.

On October 15, the Alianza proclaimed "In the Name of Almighty God" that the Pueblo República de San Joaquín del Río de Chama had "resumed all rights and authorities vested in it August 1, 1806" by King Charles IV of Spain. Tijerina led scores of followers into a Forest Service campground and announced that the City Republic had assumed jurisdiction over 600,000 acres.

When federal authorities ignored the action. Tijerina repeated the performance—and this time it was hard to ignore. Alianza members, some with guns in hand, swarmed into the

Echo Amphitheater recreation area. They confiscated government trucks and radio equipment and arrested two forest rangers. The two were tried on the spot, convicted of trespassing on San Joaquín lands, and released with a warning. This time the federal government reacted, but not with the sort of action Tijerina had hoped to provoke. Instead he and four of his lieutenants were indicted on criminal charges of assaulting federal officials and illegal seizure of government equipment.

If Tijerina was dismayed he gave no sign of it. He flew to Washington and called on the Department of State—asking the U.S. government to grant diplomatic recognition to the City State of San Joaquín. He got no further than a legal officer, who debated technicalities of the Treaty of Guadalupe Hidalgo with him. Failing an exchange of ambassadors, the Alianza began preparing for its third attempt to force the United States into a legal collision. Instead it collided, in bloody violence, with the authority of the State of New Mexico.

The developments came rapidly. On the Tierra Amarilla Land Grant the night skies were red with arson fires. Arson and fence cutting are not novelties on the nine-hundred-square-mile grant—a traditional site of violent hard feelings between Anglo ranchers and Spanish villagers—but this year it was worse than usual. Two homes burned, several barns, and so many haystacks that by late May the Rio Arriba sheriff's office wryly announced that the worst was over because there was little left to burn. Tijerina, meanwhile, was having troubles of his own. Scheduled to stand trial in July on the federal indictments, he was ordered to surrender membership lists of his organization to the court. He ignored the order, failed to answer a resulting contempt of court citation, and became a fugitive. From wherever he was hiding, he sent notices to the press announcing that his followers would rally at the Rio Arroba County village of Coyote on Saturday, June 3. Reporters, who could find Tijerina even when the law could not, quoted him as calling for a "showdown," as hinting that the Alianza would take control of the San Joaquín grant by force of arms, and as saying that his members would come to Coyote "prepared to fight." Tension mounted, and apparently with good cause.

The rumors said Alianza members were buying weapons. State Police were tipped that one Albuquerque sporting goods store had sold out its supply of carbines, plus fifteen hundred rounds of ammunition. A report arrived at the governor's office that the Alianza had obtained a case of hand grenades, three machine guns, and an unknown quantity of gas masks.

In the settlements around the contested territory, pamphlets appeared in mailboxes warning residents who were not "citizens" of San Joaquín to get out of the City State territory. Federal employees at the big Abiquiu flood control dam east of Coyote and at the Forest Service Station began sending wives and children out of the area. In the thin air of the northern New Mexico high country there was the smell of impending violence.

Friday, on the eve of the expected showdown, two men in Santa Fe moved to prevent that violence. They moved in opposite directions.

Governor David F. Cargo, a young liberal Republican whose wife had once paid Alianza dues, met with two representatives of the elusive King Tiger. He promised that if they would call off the Coyote rally he would meet publicly with Tijerina—giving him a chance to turn gracefully away from a headlong collision. But eight blocks away, District Attorney Alfonso Sanchez had called State Police officials to another meeting. Sanchez had run out of patience.

If Governor Cargo's solution was dictated by his sympathy for the plight of Alianza followers, Sanchez looked instead at the leadership and felt extreme distaste. Himself an heir to the Old Tomé, Sanchez had been convinced since 1964 that the Alianza was exploiting his people, milking the poor and the ignorant and inciting them to violate the law in a hopeless cause. While Cargo arranged his peace meeting, Sanchez was obtaining court warrants for the arrest of the King Tiger and a dozen of his top aides.

The dragnet worked through the night, with Cristoval and Anselmo Tijerina, brothers of the King Tiger, among the first arrested. By dawn nine others were in jail on charges ranging from unlawful assembly, to carrying of deadly weapons, to attempted extortion. No bond would be allowed, Sanchez said, until Saturday afternoon—after the Coyote "showdown."

As usual, the net missed Reies Tijerina, but it bagged big game. In a car stopped at a roadblock, State Police found several pistols, a sniper's rifle with telescopic sight, a portable shortwave radio, and at least part of the Alianza's supply of gas masks. Also seized during the night were copies of a book on guerrilla warfare and detailed maps of the area. Markings on these indicated that the town of El Rito was to be captured and used as headquarters and showed sites for roadblocks.

The maps seemed to indicate what morning might bring. The governor went to the Santa Fe County jail and met with Alianza leaders held there. By midnight he had persuaded them to call their families and associates urging a postponement of the Coyote meeting.

Whatever was planned for Coyote on June 3, the result was a fiasco. Alianza members driving toward the village early Saturday were met at State Police roadblocks and warned that they might be arrested and prosecuted for unlawful assembly. Many turned back. Others, aware of the happenings during the night, did not leave home. Only about eighty reached the village, to find the community swarming with newsmen and police but no leaders to tell them what to do. Rain began falling and by noon the crowd, angry and confused, drifted away.

The anger focused on the district attorney. Alfonso Sanchez had always been considered a key enemy of the movement. A warrant had already been drawn for his arrest—to be served if he appeared at the Coyote gathering. It was decided now to use this warrant. Sanchez would be arrested and brought to trial by the Pueblo República of San Joaquín on charges of violating the rights of its citizens. The opportunity would come Monday, when those arrested Friday night would be taken to the Tierra Amarilla courthouse for arraignment. The affair was arranged by the "Department of Vigilance" of the Pueblo Republic. This department selected twenty men, most of them apparently volunteers. They would be armed with rifles, carbines, and pistols and would take along a dynamite bomb. In Tierra Amarilla, sympathizers would serve as scouts.

Thus the stage was set for what Tijerina would later call "a terrible success."

Monday morning Tierra Amarilla was tense. But as the day wore on the village relaxed. The prisoners arrested Friday night arrived in two State Police cars. By 2:45, Judge James Scarborough was completing the proceedings. The defendants were to be released on bond. State Police Captain Martin Vigil called headquarters at Sante Fe, reported all quiet, and left. Another officer drove away to check on a disturbance at a sawmill—an argument over time off taken to attend Alianza meetings. Two other State policemen were called away to check an accident on U.S. Highway 84. Of the State Police detachment, that left only Nick Saiz, a tall young patrolman. Saiz stood at the lobby bulletin board, idly reading county notices. In the lobby telephone booth, UPI reporter Larry Calloway was dictating a story on the arraignment to Bureau Chief Ed McManus in Albuquerque. The Alianza leaders, freed on bond, were leaving the courthouse. Outside, the village drowsed in the sun.

At almost exactly 3:00 P.M., a red pickup truck, two sedans, and a station wagon stopped in front of the courthouse. There were nineteen or twenty men in the vehicles. Some remained outside. Others, perhaps ten or twelve, trotted up the front steps. Patrolman Saiz whirled from the bulletin board and found himself surrounded by armed men. One told him to hand over his pistol. He hesitated, then reached down to drop his weapon from its holster. The man fired at point-blank range. Saiz fell, his arm broken and a bullet through his chest. Jailer Elogio Salazar looked out of the door of the sheriff's office and saw Saiz shot and the invaders running down the hall. He shouted a warning to Sheriff Benny Naranjo and jumped through the window. As he jumped, someone outside shot him twice with a semiautomatic rifle—wounding him in the face and shoulder. The gunman, one witness said, was a boy no older than fourteen.

The "arresting party" swarmed through the courthouse. The sheriff was subdued with a blow on the head from a gun butt. The undersheriff, Dan Rivera, was knocked down with a pistol. Other raiders burst into the room where the County Commission was meeting, clubbing Deputy Pete Jaramillo and capturing the commissioners and a group of spectators. There was a flurry of gunshots. Some county employees escaped through the windows. Others were herded into the commission room, along with reporter Calloway and the sheriff. They were told to sit quietly. A young man with a bland, round face lounged against the doorsill. He held fused dynamite in one hand and a lighted cigarette in the other.

"You are very good people," he said. "Don't make us hurt you." Some of those in the room knew the young man as Baltazar Martinez, a neighbor, the son of a widow at the village of Canjilon.

Others in the arresting party ransacked the courthouse looking in vain for Alfonso Sanchez. Captives were warned to tell where he was hiding or be shot. Finally Jaramillo convinced them that the district attorney was ninety miles away at Santa Fe.

The raiders, Reies Tijerina among them, held the courthouse almost two hours. Locked doors were shot open, papers and money from the County Treasurer's vault were scattered on the floor, the sheriff's radio equipment was smashed, and all but three of the building's telephones were destroyed. Someone, probably one of the raiders, called the clinic at the neighboring village of Parkview and Saiz was rushed away in an ambulance. Another unidentified Samaritan loaded the wounded jailer into a pickup truck, drove sixty miles to the Española Valley Hospital, and left him there.

During these leisurely operations, three State policemen drove into the village. They were met by a volley of rifle fire from the courthouse and a nearby house, and abandoned their disabled cars. (None of the three was wounded, although officers later recovered thirty-three spent slugs from their vehicles.) Finally, as silently as they had come, the raiders slipped away from the building.

The last to leave were Baltazar Martinez, twenty-two, and Baltazar Apodaca, a seventy-two-year-old World War I veteran. They warned those held in the commission room not to move, ushered Jaramillo and Calloway into Jaramillo's patrol car to serve as hostages, and drove away. It was 5:00 P.M.

Martinez and Apodaca drove to Canjilon, a Carson National Forest village where a group of Alianza followers was camped. They found State Police Chief Joe Black and several of his officers waiting. Apodaca was disarmed and captured but Martinez, with his dynamite tucked in his belt and a cocked pistol held at Jaramillo's head, escaped into the forest where he released his hostage and disappeared. The other raiders had already done the same.

The lance had struck the windmill vane. From that point all else was anticlimatic.

The National Guard rushed self-propelled anti-aircraft guns and troops into the area but left behind its ammunition. (General John Jolly announced he was sending for twenty thousand rounds, which he said "wouldn't last long if we start shooting." The state's good luck at this incompetence was revealed later. During a demonstration on the University of New Mexico campus, the Guard arrived after the demonstrators had driven away, but guardsmen managed to bayonet a gaggle of curious taxpayers, including four reporters, a man in a hip cast, an ambulance attendant, and one of their own troopers.) The raiders, inevitably, were identified and arrested when they returned to their homes. Tijerina was caught the following week. He and eighteen of his members were charged with an array of felonies ranging up to first-degree kidnapping and assault to murder. And finally, when Tijerina was free again on bond, another rally was held in the Carson National Forest in which U.S. Forest Service signs were burned and Reies Lopez Tijerina again demonstrated, to any who might still doubt it, that he was indeed "a man who is not afraid."

The scene: A crowd of Alianza followers, Forest Service personnel, and State Police near Gallina. Tigerina wresting himself away from Forest Service investigator James Evans, pulling a carbine from his car, ordering Evans to "get your gunslingers out of here." And then, a frozen moment with Tijerina aiming his carbine at Evans, Evans pointing his rifle at Tijerina, State policeman Robert Gilliland and another officer aiming their weapons at the Alianza leader's head. "I thought I was going to die," Tijerina recalled later. But he didn't lower the carbine until Juan Roybal, his bodyguard, told him to.

But climactic deeds never allow successful encores. The Alianza attempted citizen arrests on the governor and others without success, and there were other secondary scenes: Tijerina among the Black Panthers, Tijerina at the Poor People's March in Washington, Tijerina in the role of darling of the radical left, Tijerina's headquarters bombed and bombed again. Tijerina serving as his own attorney and winning his own acquittal from the courthouse raid charges. Tijerina running for governor and receiving two thousand votes, and Tijerina sitting in his shabby office wait-ing to begin a three-year federal sentence for destroying Forest Service property—leaning forward across the table, his green eyes intent with the dream. The task, he said, will be completed. His people will take possession of the San Joaquín grant.

"I can see a city there. I can see our schools—our own radio station." The incredible vision was intact.

But then there are other scenes. Tijerina leaving for federal prison. The Alianza dividing over money from well-wishing church groups. Tijerina free again, a little older now, a little gray in those heavy black eyebrows. Tijerina on television talk shows, Tijerina involved with the do-good groups and the civic groups organizing Brotherhood events. And the Alianza in fractions.

In his way, Miguel Cervantes—that soothsayer of the Spanish soul—saw it all four hundred years ago. Don Quijote, too, was cured of his impossible dream.

Keeping Secrets from the Russians

1953. Cold War at its frigid worst. The age of missiles suffering through its Top-Secret birth-pangs. The United Press reporter driving down the Tularosa Basin stopped for gasoline at Three Rivers. He didn't exactly need gas. He had been driving since dawn. A while back the map had said 17 miles to Oscura, but when he had reached the place where the dot named Oscura should be there was nothing there, just a crossroads with a gravel road leading westward past the barren gray hills to some secret place on the White Sands Missile Range. And then the map said 11 miles to Three Rivers, which now proved to be nothing in the world but Shorty Miller's filling station and another 115 miles to drive down the Chihuahuan desert to El Paso. The reporter had not been over this road before, and was new to the Southern Rockies, to the miles-wide expanses of lava flow, to distant blue mountains and the sky overpowering an empty landscape and the thought, after miles of deserted highway paralleled by the deserted Southern Pacific tracks, that Planet Earth had been abandoned.

Shorty Miller, having inserted nozzle in tank, wiped the windshield, noticed the press sticker, and said where you headed?

And the reporter (stretching his legs and staring out across the basin) said he was going to Fort Bliss.

Guess you're going down there to watch them shoot off that new missile, Miller said, and the reporter looked surprised and said why yes, he guessed so, but the military types said it was so secret they wouldn't tell what they were demonstrating. Miller said well, it'll be the one they call the Wac Corporal then, and you might as well come in and have a cup of coffee because that shot's going to be postponed. Lot of trouble on that one. Supposed to go 400 miles but the best they got was 150. Burned liquid oxygen and super-cooled nitrogen mixed with the fuel and that made it colder than a well-digger's butt and the pump wouldn't work right. Anyway it wasn't working this morning. That's what the radar people said. They always stopped off for a cup on the way up to the station on Little Burro Peak and this morning it just wasn't working right, nitrogen corrosion. And the shot wasn't going to come off on time.

So the reporter sat on the stool inside and said why call it Three Rivers when there wasn't any water and Shorty said there used to be when he was a kid before it stopped raining. He poured them each a cup of coffee and they went outside again and Shorty pointed out across the basin and said nothing but creosote brush now but the first time I rode across there coming over from the Rio Grande the grass came right up to the stirrups.

Used to rain some then. But now even with the cattle all run out and it fenced off for the rocket range the grazing isn't coming back. And come to think of it, Shorty said, you could save yourself driving down to Bliss because you can stand right here at these gas pumps and see that rocket hit. Miller pointed and the heat waves weren't rising yet and the outline of the Fra Cristobal Range was sharp blue against the western horizon. Miller said right down there is where they light and sometimes the fuel tanks don't blow up but the pipes rupture and they shoot a big column of white into the sky and for several minutes it's real pretty. Different colors depending on the fuel they're experimenting with. Looks like a fountain.

When the reporter got to Fort Bliss a brigadier general came into the briefing room and interrupted the colonel and said the demonstration was going to be delayed temporarily. The reporter asked him if they planned to shoot a ballistic missile and the general said no comment. And the reporter asked if it was the one they called the Wac Corporal and the general stared at him and said all such information, including code names, was classified Secret.

9

Mr. Luna's Lazarus Act

Shortly after a recent primary election in New Mexico, a former Santa Fe city hall employee named Conway Richard Ferguson filed a breach of contract suit in district court. Mr. Ferguson alleged that a state representative whom I shall call Tomas Luna had hired him to run against Luna in the Democratic primary. He complained that Mr. Luna had not delivered the fee agreed upon for this service—a job.

To one not familiar with the intricate forms political campaigns sometimes take, such an arrangement might seem peculiar—even eccentric. Why would an officeholder hire someone to run against him? In the answer lies the story of an incident which a student of mine named Peter Kendall once called a "do-it-yourself Lazarus Act."

Mr. Kendall is a disciple of the A. J. Liebling, William Shakespeare, Col. John R. Stingo, Julia Ward Howe school of the simile, and thus his figure of speech is exactly appropriate. Politically speaking, Mr. Luna was hopelessly dead before the primary. He didn't have a prayer. And his resurrection was indeed self-induced. Like a drowned Israeli giving himself artificial respiration on the Cairo side of the Suez Canal, he could expect no help, and he got none. He restored himself solely through a virtuoso display of applied intelligence.

To appreciate Mr. Luna's feat it is necessary to understand the hideousness of his problem.

The untutored might have thought Mr. Luna's prospects for renomination to the House of Representatives looked moderately promising as the primary election approached. His only avowed opponent was Lavon McDonald, a Santa Fe football coach. Luna had defeated McDonald for the party's nomination two years earlier. He had the advantage of incumbency. And while the victory had been narrow it had served to establish Luna as a winner and McDonald as a loser. Since those in the voting booths, like those at the pari-mutuel windows, prefer to pick winners, Mr. Luna's position seemed on the surface stronger than it had been two years before.

But in politics things are seldom what they seem on the surface. Below the surface where reality dwells Mr. Luna's position was hopeless.

There were in that election year three institutions important to anyone with political aspirations in Santa Fe County. One was City Hall, with its relatively small but well-drilled cadre of payrollers. Another was the county Democratic organization which oversaw the far-flung but less disciplined county courthouse patronage. And the third was *The New Mexican*, of which I was editor at the time. It was the county's only paper, it usually championed the Democratic cause, and it influenced a good many votes in the party primary.

To win in the primary the candidate needed some sort of favorable balance among these three—for example, the support of two to offset the animosity of the other, or the vigorous support of one if both of the others were slightly worse than neutral. But in his single term representing the county in the legislature, Mr. Luna had managed to outrage *The New Mexican,* to alienate City Hall, and to lose the confidence of the party powers in the courthouse. Three strikes and you're out.

Mr. Luna's troubles were rooted in House Bill 167, which he had introduced in the past session of the legislature. He was a funeral home employee and his bill provided several minor amendments to the regulations governing licensing of embalmers. Similar measures are introduced by the dozens in every session at the behest of trade organizations, professional associations, and other special interest groups. They are called "courtesy bills" and they normally make their feeble way through the legislative labyrinth without much attention from anyone—including the lawmaker who had been talked into introducing them.

It soon became apparent to the political reporters that House Bill 167 was not a normal courtesy bill. Mr. Luna was devoting himself to its passage with a diligence grotesquely out of proportion to its importance. A curious reporter read the bill. He found that House Bill 167 did not tighten the requirements for the licensing of embalmers, but slightly relaxed them. He could have been no more surprised had he found the measure legalized grave-robbing.

To understand the reporter's amazement, and the quality of

Mr. Luna's heresy, one needs to know something of the dedication shown by New Mexico special interest groups to the protection of the public from charlatans. The embalmers, plumbers, electricians, lawyers, building contractors, and so forth, have each arranged for the passage of a law which requires a license to practice in their profession. The custom is to set qualifications for licensing at lofty levels. Those already plumbing, selling real estate, or embalming save themselves from the embarrassment of trying to meet these qualifications by having a "grandfather clause" inserted in the law. This automatically licenses anyone already on the gravy train. Thus, while the public is not exactly protected from all charlatans, it is at least guaranteed against Johnny-come-lately charlatans. Later, as newcomers gradually manage to get past the barriers, they in turn raise the requirements anew, assuring that if they have any competition it will be from men better qualified than themselves. This custom tends to insure prosperity within the trades. It also encourages New Mexico householders to say please and thank you when dealing with their plumbers and has caused a report, perhaps exaggerated, that one who qualifies for an embalmer's license in New Mexico can also qualify for admission to the American College of Surgeons.

If all this explains the reporter's surprise at Mr. Luna's attempt to lower—instead of raise—the fence protecting the embalming traffic from competition, it did not explain Mr. Luna's great interest in the bill. However, political writers felt they had found a clue to this when they learned that the revisions proposed by Mr. Luna exactly fit those required to qualify Mr. Luna himself for an embalmer's license.

In politics such a coincidence is mildly reprehensible but not seriously so. But Mr. Luna had been guilty of the more serious sin of being caught at it by the press. For a reason I can no longer recall (it may have been that, having endorsed Mr. Luna for this job, we expected him to be working on bills *we* considered important instead of on bills *he* considered important) we at *The New Mexican* took a belligerently jaundiced view of this affair. Mr. Luna was publicly castigated in surly editorials. This caused Democratic leaders at both City Hall and the county courthouse—shamans who base their superstitions on pragmatism—to begin thinking of Mr. Luna as bad luck. Mr. Luna became definitely expendable in the party's primary election.

To make matters worse, *The New Mexican* chose not to forget the incident. As editor of the Santa Fe paper at the time, I had sent word to Mr. Luna to expect editorial opposition if he chose to run again. The ploy is intended to encourage an unfavored prospect to decide not to run and, while it rarely works, it doesn't cost anything to try. In a race at this level the newspaper's effect was known to be less important than in more prominent campaigns. Still, a negative factor of perhaps four hundred voters had to be mixed into the calculations because of the paper's bellicose attitude.

On the positive side, Mr. Luna's personality rated a definite plus. He is a slender man with small bones and an intelligent, ascetic face. His smile under a narrow mustache is quick and genuine and his manner amiable. Mr. Luna is one of those individuals who genuinely likes his fellow man and it is politically fortunate for him that this shows. A mustache was considered a very slight political handicap in Santa Fe county at that time (less so in the hairy 1970s), with the antimustache element probably amounting to fewer than two votes per precinct. That's a relatively trivial number but not one overlooked by the careful candidate.

It happened that the climate of the times proved favorable to Mr. Luna's cause. It was a vintage year for politics in New Mexico. A three-man race for the Democratic gubernatorial nomination had divided the county into three nicely balanced factions. City Hall backed one contender, State Representative Bruce King and his courthouse admirers supported another, and Secretary of State Betty Fiorina and her cohort of State Capital janitors and yardmen were behind the third. To the east, both parties in San Miguel County were torn by civil war. To the north in Rio Arriba County, the perennial revolt against Democratic Chairman Emilio Naranjo was proving unusually clamorous, with the two Democratic factions contending loudly for control of the machinery for selecting election officials. The right to name these poll clerks is considered important in Rio Arriba for three reasons. One is the local adage that a vote on the tally sheet is worth two in the ballot box. Another is the fact that the U.S. Census Bureau counted 11,308 persons twenty-one or older in the county, of whom 14,878 were registered to vote. The implications of having 3,570 invisible voters on the rolls are enough to stimulate any politician. The third and most immediate reason that control of the polls seemed important lay in an incident of the past election in which certain rural polling places had shown a tendency to move around the precinct, like the elusive pea in the shell game, making it difficult for voters of the wrong persuasion to find a place to register their opinions.

With flamboyant operations under way on all sides, those who might otherwise have been watching Mr. Luna were distracted. Party leaders dedicated to his destruction were preoccupied with their own survival. *The New Mexican* had a different problem. Its readership depends on political news to approximately the same extent as that of *Playboy Magazine* depends upon bare skin. That spring was harvest time for such news and *The New Mexican* was simply too busy to torment Mr. Luna as thoroughly as it had intended. Besides, both the politicians and the newspapers could see, for reasons soon to be explained, that Mr. Luna's cause was hopelessly lost.

As filing day approached it became clear that Mr. Luna would not only be opposed by Coach McDonald, the favorite of City Hall, Sheriff M. V. (Tomato) Ortiz, who claimed fealty of the county building, was getting in the race. Since Tomato Ortiz had been picked to replace the incumbent county Democratic chairman in a planned postprimary party reorganization, he was in a position to rob Luna of what little organizational support McDonald might have left him. Worse, the sheriff was, like Luna, a member of one of those proud old many-branched Spanish colonial families that understand politics as Attila understood war and approach it with the same enthusiasm. Not only would Ortiz be a formidable opponent in himself, he would cut sharply into Luna's sources of support.

The only significant bloc of support not stripped from Mr. Luna by the combined forces opposing him was one he held as a result of his hobby. An assistant at a Santa Fe funeral home, he had served for much of his adult life as a volunteer *elogiador*, delivering the traditional oration of eulogy at countless Spanish-

American funerals. This free service had caused him to say a great many fine things about a great many deceased persons. In Santa Fe County one cannot say with complete certainty that dead people can't vote, since the names on old tombstones sometimes turn up on new voter registration lists. Whether or not Mr. Luna could count on ghostly support, he could count on the warm friendships of many survivors. These postmortem friends, scattered as they were through every precinct, gave Mr. Luna a relatively small but extremely loyal political base. This was to prove important.

Some time before the March deadline for the filing of candidacies in the May primary it is necessary for politicians to strike a careful balance of their various assets and liabilities. They must then compare their own potential performance at the polls with a sensible estimate of their opponents' popularity. If the comparison is unfavorable, they must then decide what corrective steps should be taken. It is at this point that the politician is most vulnerable. Candidates tend to err on the side of vanity, overestimate their own charm, and make fatal miscalculations. When they win the margin disappoints them. If they lose they are thunderstruck. In view of what was to happen it seems Mr. Luna avoided this pitfall. He apparently calculated with cool, impersonal accuracy that in the impending three-man race he would receive approximately 2,250 votes. Since a turnout of 7,000 was expected this would give him a third place finish in a close race and no better than a poor second under any circumstance.

To finish first, and politics gives no second prizes, Mr. Luna would need at least 2,600 votes. But he was trapped between a strong Anglo-name candidate and a strong Spanish-name contender. Further, he was barred from a bellicose campaign which might otherwise have proved effective. He must have calculated that this would attract the attention of *The New Mexican,* which would then certainly disinter House Bill 167 and expose it in the most unfavorable light. Otherwise the newspaper, preoccupied as it was with more lively affairs elsewhere, would probably satisfy itself with endorsing one of his opponents.

A less intelligent man than Mr. Luna might have calculated that if he could not win with 2,250 votes, and could not effectively increase this total, he was therefore a loser. Such a man would simply have failed to file his candidacy papers, explaining, as disappointed politicians always do, that the press of personal business made the sacrifice to public service impossible. Mr. Luna, however, carried his reasoning an important extra step. If he could not get more than 2,250 votes and could not win with this number, could he perhaps win with fewer votes? And thus Mr. Luna found his way out of an apparent dilemma on the wings of an apparent paradox.

Politicians are traditionally reticent concerning the true nature of their tactics and Mr. Luna has kept his own counsel concerning the form his calculations took. But we do know that when the county clerk's office closed on primary filing day the voter had been offered not three candidates for Mr. Luna's position, but nine.

In addition to Luna, Tomato Ortiz, and Lavon McDonald, the names Lorence, Mitchell, Goodman, and Conway Richard Ferguson would appear on the ballot. All are resoundingly Anglo in sound and shape. The names of Ludger Lucero and Arturo Garcia would also appear, names as common in the Spanish-American counties as Johnson and Jones in Texas.

These six persons, whether or not they were aware of their

role, were what the politician calls vote-splitters. Vote-splitters fall into two categories. The professional rents out his name for use on the ballot, as Mr. Ferguson indicated he had done. This type is preferred, since his behavior and the vote he will draw can be closely calculated in advance. The other sort is drawn from the ranks of those who normally stand on the sidelines, barely resisting the siren song of politics. These may be nudged into a race as dead-serious candidates, perhaps by the promise of support which will not be forthcoming. They may be persuaded to make a race for experience, knowing when they file their papers they have no real chance of winning. Both of these types were represented among the six, along with others whose motivation remains known only to themselves.

The use of these nonprofessional vote-splitters is risky business requiring cool nerves. In 1950, for example, the Democratic organization pushed the governor's chauffeur into the State Corporation Commission primary to draw votes away from a challenger who was threatening the favored incumbent. The driver, Ingram B. Pickett, was a former Keystone Cop who happened to be six feet eleven inches tall and who campaigned so vigorously that the challenger ran a poor third. But, to the terrible chagrin of the professionals, Pickett also defeated the anointed one, and New Mexico was served for twelve years by the world's tallest corporation commissioner.

Despite the quibbling of opponents, who insisted he was an inch short of the mark, Mr. Pickett had his name legally changed to "Ingram 7-Foot Pickett," removed his office door from its hinges to signify rapport with the public, and proved invincible on the ballot.

Mr. Luna has never taken public credit for masterminding the entry of the six additional candidates in the race for his legislative seat and is not likely to do so, since custom dictates modesty in such affairs. It would do him less than justice, however, to suggest that he was surprised by any of these candidacies. In view of Mr. Ferguson's postelection statements, it seems only fair to grant Mr. Luna the authorship of at least the final delicate balancing of the primary election ballot. And to grant him even this much is to grant him considerable genius. The precinct-by-precinct mathematics involved in calculating this exact human formula would tax an electronic computer.

In varying degrees each of these six vote-splitters would diminish Mr. Luna's own vote. His problem relative to Mr. McDonald was slightly less complex. Here the purpose was to cancel the effect of a group of voters whom Santa Feans call *Tejanos*. The word, a mild insult, means "Texans" but is used as a generic term for innocent and uncouth newcomers who are 100 percent Anglo. Anglo, as used in northern New Mexico, doesn't exactly mean Anglo-Saxon. It is best explained by repeating an old story which has delighted several generations of Santa Feans. It seems a Negro citizen was accosted at the Precinct Seventeen polls by a Spanish American and asked how much was being paid for votes. "I don't know," said the Negro, "they haven't got around to us Anglos yet." In other words, Anglo is a negative term meaning the person so designated is of neither Spanish nor Indian descent.

Politicians know that Tejano Anglos, if given a choice, will vote for Anglo-name candidates or, because of the usual electoral inertia, for incumbents. In the race in question, most of them would vote for the Anglo, McDonald, and some for the incumbent, Luna. Thus, while the Anglo-name vote-splitters would hurt McDonald more than Luna, they would hurt Luna more than Tomato Ortiz. Obviously, these Anglo vote-splitters could be neither underdone nor overdone.

On the other side of the scale from the Tejanos, the anti-Anglo prejudice vote had to be considered. This faction, which the politicians call the "Mexican Ku Klux Klan," would never vote for anyone with a name as Anglo as McDonald. Their motivation is historical, and easily summarized. The Anglo immigrants stole all their property. It's the same sort of grudge bankers bore against the late John Dillinger and just as hard to argue with. Mr. Luna's problem was to diminish the number of these votes which Tomato Ortiz would receive. And he couldn't split this vote too much. A slight oversolution of this end of the problem would tip the delicate balance to a McDonald victory.

One suspects that in such narrow and nerve-racking calculations Mr. Luna might have fingered his mustache and remembered the admonition of Publius Syrus that even the smallest hair casts its shadow. His victory was hairbreadth. If he had lost by the same margin it would have been almost literally by the political width of the antimustache vote.

When the returns were tabulated the night of May 8 in the smoky, crowded county clerk's office, they showed the Anglo-name splitters had lured a total of 1,053 ballots away from McDonald and Luna. The Spanish-name splitters had taken 1,341 votes away from Ortiz and Luna. Of the 4,550 votes remaining, Luna received 1,535, Ortiz, 1,524, and McDonald 1,491. State Representative Tomas Luna had been renominated by 11 votes.

A glance at the election returns makes it plain that there was no margin for mistakes. The name of the unhappy Conway Richard Ferguson, for example, attracted 228 votes. McDonald's share of these would have made him an easy winner. On the other hand, another like Ferguson in the contest, while further weakening McDonald, would certainly undercut Luna enough to cancel his 11-vote margin over Tomato Ortiz. As it was, Mr. Luna had been pared down to a point just a couple of hundred votes above the rock bottom support of his graveyard disciples.

It need only be added that while the political fraternity is stern it is also just. There was some feeling that Mr. Luna had been indiscreet again in the relationship alleged by Mr. Ferguson, since there are those available to perform such chores without calling post-facto public attention to the maneuver. But the court suit died quietly and Mr. Luna's adroitness drew the applause it deserved. Mr. Luna was no longer considered bad luck.

He defeated his Republican opponent in the November general election and two years later received his own party's supreme compliment for applied intelligence. He drew no opponent at all in the Democratic primary.

Author's Notes

These essays were written a long time ago, when I was a forty-year-old graduate student at the University of New Mexico. I was tempted to revise some of them to correct anachronisms and, frankly, because I think I've learned some writing tricks since then. However, these footnotes will be easier.

1. Bizarre as some of it seems, everything reported in the cover story is based on fact, including the Pontius Pilate Hotel mentioned in the memoirs of W. W. H. Davis. However, since the incident, Taos has converted its underground police station into tourist rest rooms and built a jail invulnerable to plastic spoons. Nothing much else has changed. For example, another Taos-style bandido has since tried to rob the same bank, demanding money while demonstration threatening kung fu chops. A state cop happened in to cash a check and collared him.

2. My old friend Alex Atcitty has gone to the reward such good men deserve. And, had I bought that $900 Two Grey Hills rug from Mr. Stock, it would now be worth about five grand.

3. Bubonic plague still claims a victim every year or so in New Mexico but Bryan Miller now looks down upon it from heaven.

4. Cletus Xywanda took his dreams of Pan-African nationalism back to Nigeria, joined his Ibibio tribesmen in their efforts to form an independent Biafra, and died with untold thousands of others when the military crushed their rebellion.

5. The isolated spot where Jerry Dawson found his Stone Age hunting site is being engulfed by Rio Rancho, where Intel builds the Pentium chips which power our computers. Readers of *Dance Hall of the Dead* will recognize Jerry's dig, but in the novel it was being worked by a totally different and fictional grad student.

6. Nothing much has changed at Las Trampas in the past thirty years (nor in the past two hundred). I pray it never will.

7. The last time I visited backstage at the Smithsonian Museum of Natural History I saw the bust of Ales Hrdlicka, its former director, in a place of honor. Nigger George McJunkin, who proved Hrdlicka's dogma of No-Early-Man-in-the-Americas was disastrous nonsense, was not represented.

8. The problem of swindled land grants still festers in the mountains of Northern New Mexico.

9. The undertaker I gave a fictitious name in the telling of "Mr. Luna's Lazarus Act" called me. He found no fault with my guesses at his political strategy but wished I had used his real name.